HENNING HAI LEE YANG was born in the Year of the Ox and says he is doomed to work hard all the time, like so many others born under this sign. He has always been interested in the art of Chinese fortune-telling and he can trace his family tree back over a thousand years to Yang Chiu Pun, one of China's most famous fortune-tellers. Although Henning Hai Lee Yang was educated as a business economist and a marine engineer, he has devoted himself to a highly successful career in Chinese fortune-telling for the last twelve years. He specializes in Chinese astrology, face-reading and feng shui. Based in Oslo, he is frequently asked to appear on radio and television programmes and is a regular contributor to newspapers and magazines.

GW00542546

The Year of the Dragon

CHINESE HOROSCOPES
FOR THE YEAR 2000

Henning Hai Lee Yang

ELEMENT

Shaftesbury, Dorset · Boston, Massachusetts
Melbourne, Victoria

© Element Books Limited 1999
Text © Henning Hai Lee Yang 1999

First published in the UK in 1999 by
Element Books Limited
Shaftesbury, Dorset SP7 8BP

Published in the USA in 1999 by
Element Books, Inc
160 North Washington Street,
Boston, MA 02114

Published in Australia in 1999 by
Element Books Limited
and distributed by Penguin Australia Limited
487 Maroondah Highway, Ringwood,
Victoria 3134

Henning Hai Lee Yang has asserted his right under the Copyright, Designs
and Patents Act, 1988 to be identified as the author of this work.

All rights reserved.
No part of this book may be reproduced or
utilized, in any form or by any means,
electronic or mechanical, without prior permission
in writing from the Publisher.

Cover design and illustration by Slatter-Anderson
Text design by Dale Tomlinson
Text illustrations by Frances Wilson
Typeset by Footnote Graphics, Warminster, Wilts
Printed and bound in Great Britain by
Biddles Limited, Guildford and King's Lynn

British Library Cataloguing in Publication data available
Library of Congress Cataloging in Publication data available

ISBN 1 86204 574 7

CONTENTS

INTRODUCTION

THE Chinese calendar is based on the movement of the moon in relation to the earth and can therefore be called a 'moon calendar'. It is the oldest system of chronological documentation in the world, dating back to the days of the Yellow Emperor, Huang Ti. Although the Chinese astrological cycles were first introduced during Huang Ti's reign in 2637 BC, the identity of the person who first developed this unique system is lost in legend.

The Chinese system seems very simple but it can be very complicated for newcomers. It can provide information about the seasons, the weather, the position of the planets and the stars, and – not least of all – the fate of each human being. It even has a special date for the beginning of spring, the day when an egg can be balanced on a smooth surface without toppling over. In Chinese this day is called 'Lap Chun', which means that the 'spring [or the egg] can stand upright' and usually occurs on 4 or 5 February. You may not believe it until you have tried it out with an egg yourself, but it is not an unusual phenomenon.

People fascinated by UFOs or extraterrestrial beings may be interested to know that ancient Chinese writings claim that the calendar system was given to us by beings from another, outer, world. Ancient Chinese objects, such as vases and household objects from the Bronze period of China, resemble those found in South America, suggesting a common source. Were there any links between Chinese and

South American cultures? Could those links have been made by beings coming down from the sky? Ancient Chinese writings say that the gods mingled with men and gave them wisdom. These gods were seated on 'dragons' and fought among themselves (there were clearly good gods and evil gods). The dragons spat fire at each other and when they were struck they fell to the ground. None of them bled but brown liquid (fuel?) came running out of them. The dragons sound as if they were flying vehicles.

Another legend tells us how and why the different years in the Chinese calendar came to have their own astrological signs. Buddha summoned all the animals on earth to a competition to swim over the Heavenly River. Only twelve animals turned up and after Buddha gave the signal to start they all jumped into the water. The Ox swam and swam, and he was in front of the other animals all of the way across. Just when he was about to climb out on to the shore at the other side, the smart Rat jumped up ahead of him. The Rat had been sitting on top of the Ox all of the time. So the smart Rat came first, the diligent Ox second and the brave Tiger third. The quiet Rabbit was fourth, then the strong Dragon was fifth. The wise Snake was sixth, the elegant Horse seventh, the artistic Goat eighth, the intelligent Monkey ninth, the colourful Rooster tenth, the loyal Dog eleventh and, finally, the lucky Pig was the last animal in the line.

Each of the signs affects every one of us – you and me, your fate and my fate. Besides the years being divided into these 12 animal signs, so are the days, the hours and even the minutes. Each year tells us how to understand the themes in our lives and months, days and minutes add their own influences. Someone familiar with the details of Chinese calendar system can interpret and compile a chart out of these influences. On the whole the details of Chinese astrological charts seem to match those of Western astrological charts, except that the Chinese charts may be slightly more accurate as they take the sex of the person into account. It is obvious that your path through life will be different depending on whether you are a man or a woman. The Western system does not go into such depth.

In this book you will learn which astrological year you are born in, and also which element influences you. This will present a better idea about who you are and teach you how to meet any challenges in your life. You should be aware that the dates of the Chinese system fall behind those of the Western system, so Chinese New Year falls after New Year in the West. In the table below you will find the corresponding dates, and you can identify your animal sign and discover the signs of your nearest and dearest. Have fun!

Chinese New Years: Date Chart

YEAR	START OF YEAR	ANIMAL SIGN	ELEMENT	ASPECT
1900	31 January	Rat	Metal	yang
1901	19 February	Ox	Metal	yin
1902	8 February	Tiger	Water	yang
1903	29 January	Rabbit	Water	yin
1904	16 February	Dragon	Wood	yang
1905	4 February	Snake	Wood	yin
1906	25 January	Horse	Fire	yang
1907	13 February	Goat	Fire	yin
1908	2 February	Monkey	Earth	yang
1909	22 January	Rooster	Earth	yin
1910	10 February	Dog	Metal	yang
1911	30 January	Pig	Metal	yin

YEAR	START OF YEAR	ANIMAL SIGN	ELEMENT	ASPECT
1912	18 February	Rat	Water	yang
1913	6 February	Ox	Water	yin
1914	26 January	Tiger	Wood	yang
1915	14 February	Rabbit	Wood	yin
1916	3 February	Dragon	Fire	yang
1917	23 January	Snake	Fire	yin
1918	11 February	Horse	Earth	yang
1919	1 February	Goat	Earth	yin
1920	20 February	Monkey	Metal	yang
1921	8 February	Rooster	Metal	yin
1922	28 January	Dog	Water	yang
1923	16 February	Pig	Water	yin
1924	5 February	Rat	Wood	yang
1925	24 January	Ox	Wood	yin
1926	13 February	Tiger	Fire	yang
1927	2 February	Rabbit	Fire	yin
1928	23 January	Dragon	Earth	yang
1929	10 February	Snake	Earth	yin
1930	30 January	Horse	Metal	yang
1931	17 February	Goat	Metal	yin
1932	6 February	Monkey	Water	yang
1933	26 January	Rooster	Water	yin
1934	14 February	Dog	Wood	yang
1935	4 February	Pig	Wood	yin
1936	24 January	Rat	Fire	yang
1937	11 February	Ox	Fire	yin
1938	31 January	Tiger	Earth	yang
1939	19 February	Rabbit	Earth	yin
1940	8 February	Dragon	Metal	yang
1941	27 January	Snake	Metal	yin
1942	15 February	Horse	Water	yang

YEAR	START OF YEAR	ANIMAL SIGN	ELEMENT	ASPECT
1943	5 February	Goat	Water	yin
1944	25 January	Monkey	Wood	yang
1945	13 February	Rooster	Wood	yin
1946	2 February	Dog	Fire	yang
1947	22 January	Pig	Fire	yin
1948	10 February	Rat	Earth	yang
1949	29 January	Ox	Earth	yin
1950	17 February	Tiger	Metal	yang
1951	6 February	Rabbit	Metal	yin
1952	27 January	Dragon	Water	yang
1953	14 February	Snake	Water	yin
1954	3 February	Horse	Wood	yang
1955	24 January	Goat	Wood	yin
1956	12 February	Monkey	Fire	yang
1957	31 January	Rooster	Fire	yin
1958	18 February	Dog	Earth	yang
1959	8 February	Pig	Earth	yin
1960	28 January	Rat	Metal	yang
1961	15 February	Ox	Metal	yin
1962	5 February	Tiger	Water	yang
1963	25 January	Rabbit	Water	yin
1964	13 February	Dragon	Wood	yang
1965	2 February	Snake	Wood	yin
1966	21 January	Horse	Fire	yang
1967	9 February	Goat	Fire	yin
1968	30 January	Monkey	Earth	yang
1969	17 February	Rooster	Earth	yin
1970	6 February	Dog	Metal	yang
1971	27 January	Pig	Metal	yin

YEAR	START OF YEAR	ANIMAL SIGN	ELEMENT	ASPECT
1972	15 February	Rat	Water	yang
1973	3 February	Ox	Water	yin
1974	23 January	Tiger	Wood	yang
1975	11 February	Rabbit	Wood	yin
1976	31 January	Dragon	Fire	yang
1977	18 February	Snake	Fire	yin
1978	7 February	Horse	Earth	yang
1979	28 January	Goat	Earth	yin
1980	16 February	Monkey	Metal	yang
1981	5 February	Rooster	Metal	yin
1982	25 January	Dog	Water	yang
1983	13 February	Pig	Water	yin
1984	2 February	Rat	Wood	yang
1985	20 February	Ox	Wood	yin
1986	9 February	Tiger	Fire	yang
1987	29 January	Rabbit	Fire	yin
1988	17 February	Dragon	Earth	yang
1989	6 February	Snake	Earth	yin
1990	27 January	Horse	Metal	yang
1991	15 February	Goat	Metal	yin
1992	4 February	Monkey	Water	yang
1993	23 January	Rooster	Water	yin
1994	10 February	Dog	Water	yang
1995	31 January	Pig	Wood	yin
1996	19 February	Rat	Fire	yang
1997	7 February	Ox	Fire	yin
1998	28 January	Tiger	Earth	yang
1999	16 February	Rabbit	Earth	yin
2000	5 February	Dragon	Metal	yang
2001	24 January	Snake	Metal	yin
2002	12 February	Horse	Water	yang

YEAR	START OF YEAR	ANIMAL SIGN	ELEMENT	ASPECT
2003	1 February	Goat	Water	yin
2004	22 January	Monkey	Wood	yang
2005	9 February	Rooster	Wood	yin
2006	29 January	Dog	Fire	yang
2007	18 February	Pig	Fire	yin

The Five Elements

At the dawn of time, there were two opposite forces, the yin and the yang, the feminine and the masculine. At another stage, these forces were each divided into five elements. In the Western style of thinking, there are only four elements, though the Chinese system has five. The five elements are not static compounds, but can be seen as powers in activity, out in nature.

We have sixty different types of animal signs, as each sign contains five different element types, reflecting the different qualities that each of these animal signs possesses, and can be modified or enforced by your very own element. The five elements exert a strong influence on you at different times of the year, except for Earth, which maintains its influence throughout the year. Wood has its highest influence during the spring, Fire around the summer, Metal around the autumn, and Water during the winter. When you identify your animal sign, you can also find out which element affects you. If you were born in 1949, then your animal sign is the Ox, and your element for that particular year is Earth.

WOOD

This element belongs to the morning and the spring. Your qualities are beauty, chastity and elegance. Wood represents the creative force and fantasy. You who are born in the element can become a poet, artist or farmer. You are probably tall and slim, and have beautiful eyes and small hands and feet. Dark skin is a lucky sign for you, too much light skin is unfortunate, as light or bright colours suggest Metal, and in this case the Metal can hurt the Wood in you.

Wood governs the liver and the eyes. The lucky colours are green or blue.

Fire

This element belongs to the middle of the day and the summer. Your qualities are beauty, happiness and joy, and Fire can also be associated with suffering, heat and clairvoyance. You are an active soldier and a leader. Fire often gives you a reddish skin, the nose of an eagle and hairiness. It is not good to be too fat or to have ears that are too big, as these indicators mean that you have too much Water in you, and that it will extinguish the Fire.

Fire rules the heart and the blood, and its colour is red.

Earth

This element belongs to the afternoon, and summer's hottest days, although it influences all the other elements throughout the year. Your qualities are fruitfulness and endurance, carefulness and strategic thinking. Earth also represents realism and hard work – elements of the businessman. Typical features are strong eyebrows and a flat stomach. You must avoid having too strong a beard and long hair. Reddish skin is a lucky sign, as it stands for Fire, which provides ashes – and Earth.

Earth rules the spleen and the mouth. The colour is yellow.

Metal

This element belongs to the evening and the autumn. Your qualities are decisiveness and ambition in reaching your goals. You can also be destructive, which can lead to total ignorance. Furthermore Metal represents strength and stubbornness. Under this element one can find the best lawyers and politicians. You have fine and even teeth, a square face and small hands.

Metal governs the lungs and the skin. The colour of Metal is white.

WATER

This element belongs to the night and the winter. Coolness and peace are typical qualities for you. Water also represents fruitfulness and force, but it is countermeasured by strong self-constraint. This element suits the artist and the businessman. The element gives strong and big hands, very thick lips and curly hair. A strong nose-tip and diffused eyes are unfortunate. Try also to avoid becoming too fat, which can lead to infertility.

Water rules the kidneys and the ears. The associated colours are black and dark blue.

How to Choose Your Partner

Selecting the right partner requires a deep understanding of Chinese astrology and the elements that influence the birthdays of the persons involved. The Chinese have a golden rule in order to give you some indication. Generally speaking, four years', eight years' and twelve years' difference between the parties will make a relationship work out well. However, gaps of three years, six years and nine years between the parties represent difficulties and disappointment in the relationship.

The Chinese are superstitious. They believe in the Dragon as the national symbol, a sign of power and strength. People born under this sign are splendid and magnificent, and achieving things in a Dragon year will also lead to good luck, harmony and wealth. No wonder most people would like to get married in the Year of the Dragon. It is also a custom for couples to marry at the beginning of the year so that they can aim to conceive and have a baby born in the Year of the Dragon too.

This is a sign of great gifts. From oracle to overlord, from pop star to millionaire, the Dragon can turn his dexterous hand to whatever he chooses. The ace up the Dragon's sleeve is nothing more or less than absolute self-belief. He possesses extraordinary willpower, which he manages to pass on to others. Children born in this sign can be very gifted as you can already understand from my description.

The Year of the Dragon is lucky for most of us, so if you have a prospective partner you should just go and get married. However, if you (or your partner) are born in the Year of the Dog or the Year of the Tiger, then you should wait until the Horse comes along, else it could create complications, as the Dog and the Tiger are deadly enemies of the Dragon.

THE RAT
You will find interesting and stable relationships with the Dragon, the Monkey, the Snake or the Ox. There will be good communication, and much love and respect for each other. You must stay away from the Rabbit and the Horse, as they are always fighting against you.

THE OX
You will find the ideal partner in the Rooster. You will also understand that the Snake, the Rat, the Rabbit or the Pig also function well together with you. However, stay away from the Tiger or the Goat, as their problems will bother you.

THE TIGER
You like to spend time with the Horse or the Dog, but you will have a very stormy relationship with the Dragon. Otherwise you will have to watch our for the Ox, the Snake or the Monkey, as they will tease you and make problems. The Pig will, however, give you great strength and joy.

THE RABBIT

The Rabbit suits the Goat or the Dog. Furthermore, you will enjoy harmonious relationships with the Pig or the Ox. Someone born under the sign of the Rooster or the Snake will just provoke you, so it is wise to keep away from these.

THE DRAGON

You fill find much joy and luck together with the Rat, the Rooster or the Monkey, because you think they are attractive and charming. Especially, the male Dragon will feel very attracted to the female Snake. Try to avoid the pessimistic Dog or the angry Tiger; if you do so, you are all right.

THE SNAKE

You will be happy with the Ox or the Rooster, but you will find it difficult to understand the Tiger, the Rabbit or the Pig. A partnership between you and another Snake will be especially tough and difficult.

THE HORSE

You should invest your relationship in a Goat, a Tiger or a Dog. The Pig will also be a good match, as you have much in common. Otherwise try to keep yourself away from the Rat or the Rooster, as you will find them bothersome.

THE GOAT

You will be satisfied to encounter and settle down with a Rabbit, a Pig or a Horse. A Dog will make you worry all the time. Otherwise a relationship with a Pig will be harmonious and give you positive impulses. You enjoy the company of a Pig.

THE MONKEY

You will find the Dragon or the Rat very attractive; it might even be love at first sight. Otherwise you will have to keep yourself out of the reach of the claws of the Tiger or the poisonous teeth of the Snake. They will certainly make hell break out for you if you are careless.

THE ROOSTER

You fancy the Ox or the Snake, but a relationship with the Dragon will provide security. You will find the Rabbit or the Horse difficult to spend time with, and you especially find the Rat too smooth-tongued and dishonest.

THE DOG

A relationship with a Tiger will give you the excitement you need and the Horse can take you to whole new realms of experience. Life with the Rabbit will be harmonious but quiet. A future with a Dragon or a Goat will create many problems. This is not promising. Otherwise try to ally yourself with a Pig, in a relationship that will be very fruitful.

THE PIG

You think the Rabbit, the Horse or the Goat are good companions, but you should choose the Goat among these signs, as the Goat always knows how to treat a Pig. On the contrary, you should avoid the poisonous teeth of the Snake, as your life will be turned totally upside-down.

Millennium 2000: The Year of the Dragon

The Dragon is the symbol of luck and happiness in China. It was also a symbol of the Chinese Emperors in ancient times. The Chinese discovered that people born in the Year of the Dragon automatically have the same influence as the Dragon itself. Everything is big and colourful in the year of this sign. Asians, especially the Chinese, are most aware of the significance of giving birth to their babies in the Year of the Dragon.

In 1988, which was also a Dragon year representing wealth and happiness, more than 70,000 babies were born in Hong Kong. The figure is usually less than 30,000. The Hong Kong Chinese are keen practitioners of old Chinese culture and believers in Chinese superstition. Not only did the year correspond to the Year of the Dragon, but the number 88, which is associated with fortune, was a further good sign for that particular year. Since most Chinese are materialistic, they loved 1988 even more. The elder statesman of modern China, Deng Xiaoping, was a Dragon, and in 1976 he started his 'Open Door' policy towards the West, transforming China into a wealthier society than ever before. In many ways China prospered under his rule, and he was 93 years old when he died in 1997. All these events could only be explained by one thing: people born under the Year of the Dragon bring along prosperity, wealth and long life.

The Dragon is employed in great festivities to celebrate a coming New Year. The dance of the Dragon is experienced in different Chinese societies around the whole world. It symbolizes the old year about to pass away; it is time to say farewell. An even better year lies ahead.

New discoveries will usually take place in the Year of the Dragon. In 1940 the American Donald Kerst invented a machine – Betatron – that could make electrons fly at the speed of light. This and similar machines have been very useful for many atomic scientists. In another Dragon year, 1952, the American chemists Stanley and Harold Urey managed to send electronic currents through gasses that probably existed on Earth more than 5 billion years ago, proving the theory that life's building cubes came into being by themselves within the gasses. Two other American genetic researchers managed to prove that the DNA molecule that contains genes and decides our appearance is written in the same 'language' in all living creatures.

Great happenings and festivities always occur in the Year of the Dragon. The New Year will often begin with news of a major or exciting event: in the early days of 1928, Corinth was destroyed by an earthquake. In 1952 King George VI died. In 1976 the first supersonic passenger jet plane, Concorde, started its flights from Europe to the United States. More excitingly, two American space probes, Viking I and Viking II, landed on Mars in the very same year. In January 2000 the biggest international space station, ISS, will be in operation, with three astronauts on board, a huge project backed by 16 nations worldwide. The intention is for man himself to reach Mars.

Innovations within entertainment also fall into the Year of the Dragon. In 1928 the Scotsman John Logie Baird patented a technique to produce TV pictures in colour. In 1964 the Beatles sold 1 million copies of their album long before they were even placed in the shops. The most famous Beatle, John Lennon, was also born in the Year of the Dragon. And hopefully this book of mine will also reach millions of readers!

After 1999, a rather calm Year of the Rabbit, but one with some financial turmoil across the globe, it is time for more action in the Year of the Dragon 2000. It has been speculated that worldwide computer systems will break down between 31 December 1999 and 1 January 2000 as a result of the 'Millennium Bug' but I am sure the world will survive and we are headed for a prosperous year when the Metal Dragon takes over on 5 February 2000. In Chinese thinking Metal relates to prosperity and fortune. Many Asian governments around the world, and even the individual on the street, have allocated money to celebrate this special year as mankind enters the first Dragon Year of the 21st century.

This is also an exciting year for space development. We will witness several profound advancements in bringing men into space. New programmes will be launched, and space stations or even moon stations will be worked on during this particular year.

Research in fighting different diseases will experience breakthroughs in the Year of the Dragon. There will be new answers in the fight against AIDS and cancer. New medicines will help mankind to live longer and also establish a better quality of life. Doom-mongers have found little to echo to their apocalytic alarms. Many environmentalists have been convinced that scarce resources will be fought for and that prices will rise rocket high in the years to come. This is not the truth. Most of the raw materials that were supposedly dwindling show greater reserves now than they did two decades ago, as shown by the overproduction of oil and gas in 1998 and 1999. Reports from the UN reveal that even the world food supply has been increasing faster than the population it has to support. War might occur in the Year of the Dragon, but it will occur on a local scale. Our planet will no longer be threatened with nuclear annihilation. World powers will come to an understanding concerning the ban of nuclear weapons.

New systems in worldwide communication will also have a strong impact, with new tools and devices helping us to contact our neighbours in different countries in a faster and safer way. The application of mini-mobile telephones with TV, Internet, fax and video facilities will become more common during this special year. Scientists will even be working on the methods of beaming objects from one place to another in a fraction of a second. Breakthroughs will be made; sooner or later we will be able to travel at the speed of light.

Politically there might be changes here and there, and the United States will hold a presidential election this year. Clinton, who is a Dog, will step down, but he must avoid difficulties before handing over his power to a new president, as the Year of the Dragon does not promise well for people born in the Year of the Dog. Al Gore, the Vice-President, who is a Rat, will have a great chance to succeed his predecessor, as the Rat will have great success in the Year of the Dragon.

With regard to the five elements – Earth, Fire, Wood, Metal and Water – as the Chinese always think that the Dragon can fly in the sky or swim in the sea, so the Chinese link the Dragon with aspects of water or say that the Dragon can spit fire from the sky, such as thunder. The Dragon has so much in common with Fire. We have to note that the biggest coal fields in the world were opened at Selby in England in 1976. On 29 December 1940 London was being hit by Hitler's firebombs. Many beautiful churches, and the Guildhall, were burned to ashes. There will be many fireworks and bonfires in the last hours of the Year of the Dragon. Though the flames may be extinguished this time, you can be sure that when the next Dragon year arrives a new round of fireworks will start to burn again.

The
Animal Signs

THE SIGN OF THE
Rat

The Chinese name for the Rat: Shu
The first sign in the Chinese zodiac
The hours governed by the Rat: 11pm – 1am
The corresponding sign in the Western zodiac: Aquarius
Element: Water
The direction of the pole: Positive

*

The Year of the Rat in the Western Calendar

31 January 1900–18 February 1901 Metal Rat
18 February 1912–5 February 1913 Water Rat
5 February 1924–24 January 1925 Wood Rat
24 January 1936–10 February 1937 Fire Rat
10 February 1948–28 January 1949 Earth Rat
28 January 1960–14 February 1961 Metal Rat
15 February 1972–2 February 1973 Water Rat
2 February 1984–19 February 1985 Wood Rat
19 February 1996–6 February 1997 Fire Rat

Famous People Born Under the Sign of the Rat

Ursula Andress, Prince Andrew, Louis Armstrong, Shirley Bassey, Irving Berlin, Marlon Brando, George Bush, Jimmy Carter, James Callaghan, Prince Charles, Maurice Chevalier, Doris Day, Benjamin Disraeli, Clark Gable, Hugh Grant, Vaclav Havel, Charlton Heston, Gene Kelly, Glenda Jackson, Kris Kristofferson, Gary Lineker, Franz Joseph Haydn, Sean Penn, Burt Reynolds, Yves St Laurent, Lawrence of Arabia, Mark Phillips, Wolfgang Amadeus Mozart, Robert Mugabe, Olivia Newton-John, Queen Elizabeth the Queen Mother, William Shakespeare, Tommy Steele, Donna Summer, Leo Tolstoy, Pope John Paul II, Jules Verne, Andrew Lloyd Webber, Kim Wilde, Emile Zola.

The Rat in a Nutshell

POSITIVE QUALITIES
You are charming, friendly, quick-witted, flexible, intelligent, imaginative, energetic, observant and considerate.

NEGATIVE QUALITIES
Calculating, impulsive, egotistic, naïve, manipulating, over-ambitious and greedy.

CAREER SUGGESTIONS
Entertainer, journalist, politician, writer or any kind of work where you can apply your charm and capable tongue.

Main Features of the Rat

You are charming, positive and quick to see opportunities. You can also be too hasty in changing your mind and seem to be a little speculative. Others will find you somewhat unstable and opportunistic.

LUCK
You know how to appreciate the small things in life, and you are extremely fond of your close ones. The greatest chance of

finding luck occurs when somebody understands you and gives you support.

MONEY

You are clever to save and take care of what you have. You can even be very popular and famous as a result. An unimportant hobby can be very lucrative.

WORK

You are very fond of people. Sometimes you detest loneliness. Your life is colourful and you know how to make good friends. Any kind of work connected with people appeals to you.

SOCIAL LIFE

You are curious and always on the lookout for excitement. You enjoy being the centre of celebrations but you have to feel comfortable with the people around you before you will let loose. Whatever your means you love to enjoy life to the full.

BUSINESS

You are sharp, with many well-held opinions, and you see many possibilities around you. Now and then, you have a tendency to be too smart, so you might cheat yourself without knowing it.

LOVE

You are romantic and sentimental. Furthermore, you care for those you love. Your charming personality makes you the master of flirting, and this will be noticed. Few can withstand your fatal charm.

PARENTS

You are probably blessed with caring and considerate parents, but they might be too demanding, as they tend to know that you will succeed in life.

SISTERS AND BROTHERS

You have a good relationship with your siblings, and there is much love and understanding between you.

CHILDREN

You are very fond of children, and can even be rather childish yourself. You will have many children with your partner, and your children will learn how to appreciate you.

TRAVEL
You love travelling. You are especially fond of nightlife and you like to investigate its many facets on your own.

HEALTH
You have good health. You tend to be rather robust and are strong in the face of illness or disease. People born in this sign have great endurance. You will live a long life.

INVESTMENTS
Your investments are often very successful, if you are not too greedy. You are a very talented money-maker, and you will have the chance of getting very rich.

TALENTS
You are smart and clever in finding solutions to your problems. You are very diplomatic and know how to behave yourself. You can also be rather generous, though fortunately you do not spend your money without purpose.

PROSPECTS
If you manage to take care of the people who are close to you, then you will be sure that you will have a good life that is not boring. You take every day as a new challenge with a lot of possibilities.

What Kind of Rat Are You?

WOOD RAT 1924, 1984
This is a house Rat who spends much time in the loft. You are enterprising and wise, but perhaps a little restless, so you might not quite manage to stay on course. At the beginning, life can be somewhat stormy, but you will steer into more peaceful waters later on.

THE FIRE RAT 1936, 1996
This is the Rat who lives in the rice fields. You are intelligent and grave, but you tend to be rather authoritative also. At the beginning life will not be easy for you, but you will win footholds step by step. Your old age will be fine and without problems.

THE EARTH RAT 1948, 2008
This is a Rat who finds himself in a warehouse storing rice, where there is more than enough food and protection. You know

how to make use of your talents. You will live a long life without worries.

The Metal Rat 1900, 1960

This is the Rat who thrives indoors. You like to administer and help the people close to you. You will have a good life with few worries and without great danger. Your partner will appreciate your efforts and love you dearly.

The Water Rat, 1912, 1972

This is a mountain Rat. Problems have a tendency to arise when you are young, but luckily things will work out all right for you. There are great chances that you will have a successful marriage, and in time you will make good money. In any circumstances you will have to manage on your own, because you will not get any help from outsiders.

The Ascendants of the Rat

11pm–1am: the Hour of the Rat 'Zi'

You are deadly charming and very conceited. You are also very fond of your family life and take good care of the people around you. You are curious and could be a very good writer if you want to.

1am–3am: the Hour of the Ox 'Zhou'

Somewhat restless, you can be very grave at times. Of course you will be dominated by the speculative manner of the Rat, but this will be outweighed by the security the Ox provides.

3am–5am: the Hour of the Tiger 'Yin'

You can be rather bossy and aggressive. Sometimes you can be more enthusiastic than is necessary. Everything will work out right if you manage to keep an eye on your money, because you can be very generous and at times too reckless and careless in spending your money.

5am–7am: the Hour of the Rabbit 'Mao'

You are willing to learn and experience, but you might be rather difficult to understand because of the Rat in you. The charm from the Rat combined with the Rabbit's cunning will make you rather invincible.

7AM–9AM: THE HOUR OF THE DRAGON 'ZHEN'

A Rat with great ambition and a generous heart, which sometimes might even be bigger than your wallet. You will lend money to the needy without conditions, something you might regret later on. The strong will of the Dragon and the economic talents of the Rat will make you very successful in business.

9AM–11AM: THE HOUR OF THE SNAKE 'SI'

You will have a bundle of admirers. You will sneak yourself into others' wallets, as well into the hearts of others. The Snake will make you deadly charming and dangerous to spend time with, and you can be rather ruthless.

11AM–1PM: THE HOUR OF THE HORSE 'WU'

You are a true adventurer, someone willing to try many things, though they might prove to be rather risky. Your unstable nature gets you into turbulent waters concerning love. Your life is never dull. You are either on the top of the world or down in the dumps.

1PM–3PM: THE HOUR OF THE GOAT 'WEI'

You are very sentimental. You can be very fond of money, but fortunately you will combine this with good taste and refinement. Since both signs are rather opportunistic, you are masterful at hanging on to people who are influential with money and power.

3PM–5PM: THE HOUR OF THE MONKEY 'SHEN'

This a very enterprising combination. You know every trick in the book and are willing to make use of them all. With the influence of the Monkey, you are less sentimental and possess a rather humorous streak.

5PM–7PM: THE HOUR OF THE ROOSTER 'YU'

You are extra-intelligent and very skilful, but at the same time you tend to be very conceited. The Rat in you is occupied with saving your money, but the Rooster in you has many ideas on how to dispose of it. Maybe it is wise to find a job where you can use your talents to run a business with other people's money.

7PM–9PM: THE HOUR OF THE DOG 'XU'

The Dog in you wants to be righteous and impartial, but the Rat in you could not care less that you might acquire money at the expense of the conscience of the Dog. This is also a good combination for you to become a famous writer or a journalist with a sharp pen.

9pm–11pm: the Hour of the Pig 'Hai'

The Rat hates to bear the scruples of the Pig in himself. This makes you rather hesitant when you could have applied the possibilities at the favourable moment. Unless you learn how to be smarter you will end up as a charitable worker who receives no thanks for your labours.

The Year Ahead

You are a vital and happy person, intelligent and popular. You love life and have an astonishing way of making friends. Your close ones feel well in your presence. Because of your intelligence and wisdom, you are often asked for advice. People have the tendency to come to you with their problems and secrets. No wonder you like to work hard in order to achieve your goals. At the same time, you are very original and never run out of ideas.

It is a pity that you often lack the drive and the self-assurance to get these ideas working. If you can build up your self-esteem when you are young, then there are great chances for you to go far in life.

You are very observant and love to note down all the events that are happening around you. Many famous writers and journalists are born under this sign. You like work that brings you into contact with people and the media. Your way of finding yourself out of trouble makes you sought after as a consultant.

However you might be rather self-interested and egotistic. You love to be the centre of attention, but you can be rather mean and pedantic if you find yourself in bureaucratic and tight surroundings. You are quick to grasp any opportunity, which is certain to improve your standard of living. But remember: you can make yourself many enemies if you think only of yourself.

Generally you possess a good sense and feeling about money, and you are fond of it. Now and then you may act rather meanly, because you like to keep the money in your own pocket. You are crazy about collecting things, and seldom throw things away. Your home might look like a warehouse or a museum. The Rat likes to take care of his family, and you can be generous with your partner, children and close friends, as well as exceptionally loyal to your parents. And you often like to spend quite a lot of money on yourself too. As sometimes you tend to be mean and greedy, you never say no to a free dinner or a gratis ticket to a special event. Often you say yes to people who might have doubts, and you engage yourself in their businesses. You should try to keep yourself away from such speculative enterprises.

You are very articulate, but you must be aware that sometimes you tend to be overly blunt or indiscreet. Intrigue and gossip belong in your daily life. A revealing conversation will have a positive influence on you. Furthermore, you are smart at making use of any confidential influence to your own benefit. You are also clever at giving impartial advice. You are so charming and irresistible that most people will forgive your total lack of discretion.

You can look forward to an exciting and prosperous year in 2000. There will be no lack of opportunities concerning love and career. You will especially be making very good money on all your projects when you are self-employed. And when you are working for others, then a promotion and higher pay will not be far off in this profitable year. Though this year will give you excellent prospects at every angle, you will need to take care not to be exploited by others in order to avoid problems that might arise at a later stage. You will be on the go all the time, and you will have the opportunity to make friends with some very important people.

In order to achieve the best results amid all these opportunities, the Rat will have to decide what to go for this year. Determination and a positive attitude will bring rewarding results. The summer months will be especially interesting. You will have the chance for romance if you are not tied already. If you want further children, this time will also be ideal. A Dragon child will especially give you much joy and luck in the years to come.

Week By Week For People Born Under the Sign of the Rat

5–11 FEBRUARY 2000 (5 FEBRUARY: CHINESE NEW YEAR – YEAR OF THE DRAGON)

You begin the year with an easy-going week, free of problems. Chances are you might have a bit of a hangover at the start of the week, the result of New Year celebrations. You will be glad to use spare time to rest and get into better shape. This is not a good week for taking any chances. It would be unwise to speculate or gamble.

Your lucky numbers this week: 3, 4, 26, 37.

12–18 FEBRUARY 2000

Caution is required when operating anything mechanical or electrical. There is danger of accidents. Be very careful about trying out any new gadget you may not understand. Read the instructions carefully before tampering with unfamiliar equipment. The best part of the week is from Wednesday onwards. You will not want to stray far from home – something of a change for you.

Your lucky numbers this week: 1, 16, 27, 28.

19–25 FEBRUARY 2000

This is rather a strenuous period so do not try to complete important business deals this week. It will be difficult to contact or communicate effectively with influential people and any kind of celebration will have a negative impact on your work. People at your place of employment will be congenial enough, but will lack the necessary driving force to get anything going. The week is best used for jobs you can handle alone, especially those that require extra concentration. It is also good for improving your relationship with your loved ones.

Your lucky numbers this week: 12, 23, 30, 32.

26 FEBRUARY–3 MARCH 2000

You have to be on your toes this week. A quick-witted person, you are not usually taken in by other people, but someone you think you can trust may be out to deceive you in one way or another. A longstanding colleague may wish to borrow money but do not lend cash without knowing exactly when you are going to get it back and how payment will be made. If you do not cover yourself, you could end up as the loser. Devote some time to creative work that gives you an opportunity to make good use of your active imagination.

Your lucky numbers this week: 1, 22, 27, 30.

4 –10 MARCH 2000

Money matters require cautious handling. Rats must be cautious regarding people with whom they have financial dealings.

Speculation in any form would be most hazardous. You will have a tendency to be careless with money. Keep personal spending within reasonable limits and guard your wallet.

Your lucky numbers this week: 13, 24, 25, 34.

11–17 MARCH 2000

You need to slow down. You may be too anxious to move about, but think carefully on what this will achieve. Do not travel to see influential people unless you have a definite appointment. Much time and expense could be wasted journeying around this week, so conduct business by telephone wherever possible. Be more tactful in handling family matters, and watch your temper. Do not say anything in the heat of a moment that you would immediately regret.

Your lucky numbers this week: 1, 12, 20, 23.

18–24 MARCH 2000

This quiet week gives you the opportunity to plan future moves. There is unlikely to be any great pressure from above at this time. No new problems will develop in your regular job, and everything connected with routine should progress at a steady rate. This is an excellent week for giving free rein to your natural talents.

Your lucky numbers this week: 4, 15, 26, 27.

25–31 MARCH 2000

Seek knowledge helpful to your creative work. This is a good week for anything that does not require a great deal of co-operation from outsiders. Much of value can be learned by visiting a library, museum or similar place of learning. At the end of the week a sudden health problem could cause you to cancel a weekend social event.

Your lucky numbers this week: 1, 3, 16, 30.

1 APRIL–7 APRIL 2000

Make an effort to contact people who may help in furthering your career. If you have your mind set on a creative profession remember it is essential to make the best possible use of personal introductions. People who matter are likely to favour you this week, and you should have no difficulty projecting your personality in a likeable manner. A recent investment should begin paying off now.

Your lucky numbers this week: 2, 14, 25, 27.

8–14 APRIL 2000

Coupled with the events of last week, you should be able to look back on things with some satisfaction. Bear in mind that this is not a particular good period for romance, and that you could waste valuable time chasing rainbows. Stick to matters connected to work. Accept invitations to social happenings where you can rub shoulders with the rich and the influential.

Your lucky numbers this week: 1, 12, 13, 28.

15–21 APRIL 2000

You may not be thinking straight about money. It would be extremely dangerous to make new investments now; business propositions must be carefully investigated. Expert advice will cost little and could eliminate the possibility of loss if you act on your own. Be wary about getting too deeply involved with people you meet for the first time. Try to avoid becoming too emotional.

Your lucky numbers this week: 1, 2, 16, 27.

22–28 APRIL 2000

Speculation could still be your downfall. The temptation to invest in the propositions suggested by friends will be very strong. Keep your impulses in check. It is wise to look before you leap. At times of uncertainty, consult your partner in need of advice. Single Rats will find a romantic period this week.

Your lucky numbers this week: 12, 23, 24, 30.

29 APRIL–5 MAY 2000

Opposition to your plans from your partner will be difficult to understand. The actions of loved ones may appear totally illogical to you. It would best not to get involved in family disputes with people who are acting impulsively. This is a perfect week for getting down to the essentials of work and business. Deal with priorities. Romance will be exciting; someone you date for the first time is likely to turn out to be more than a ship passing in the night.

Your lucky numbers this week: 1, 7, 18, 20.

6–12 MAY 2000

You may have to alter your plans for this week in order to avoid serious arguments. Although you might feel that people are behaving irrationally, they will be calling the tune. Co-operation will be difficult to obtain. However, this is a good week for jobs that give you an opportunity to show your artistic prowess, especially if you can handle them alone.

Your lucky numbers this week: 11, 13, 25, 28.

13–19 MAY 2000

Use brain rather than brawn this week. Additional money can be made through increased mental activity rather than physical energy. Creative enterprises can be made more valuable by joining forces with people with specialized knowledge that you appear to lack. There will be no need to go it alone. This is an excellent week for teamwork on any level.

Your lucky numbers this week: 1, 13, 24, 27.

20–26 MAY 2000

Travel should be postponed this week as this is not a good time for making long journeys, whether for business or pleasure. If you cannot avoid travel this week, then be particularly cautious if driving. Take no risks on the roads. Check your car before setting out, especially tyre pressure.

Your lucky numbers this week: 2, 3, 14, 17.

27 MAY–2 JUNE 2000

An extremely happy week for activities in and around the home. There will be good opportunities to improve your relationship with your partner. Differences that have been glossed over can now be talked out to everybody's benefit. An engagement this week is likely to lead to a happy marriage.

Your lucky numbers this week: 11, 16, 28, 32.

3–9 JUNE 2000

You will have some difficulty understanding the impulsive actions of loved ones. Plans you were keen to carry out about your home may not be acceptable to them. It is also possible that someone is trying to fool you. Employment affairs will be relatively simple compared to the domestic situation. This is a good week for experimenting with new working styles.

Your lucky numbers this week: 1, 16, 22, 24.

10–16 JUNE 2000

It is quite likely that the problems of loved ones will interfere with your own plans. A member of your family may not be feeling too well so it might be necessary to cancel reservations. Do not be disappointed if entertainment you have been looking forward to for some time has to be postponed at the last minute at the weekend.

Your lucky numbers this week: 1, 11, 16, 20.

17–23 JUNE 2000

If you can keep impulsive tendencies in check, this will be a good week for business. You must watch your extravagant streak. If you play your cards right, you could increase your earnings considerably in the not too distant future. A more romantic week than usual will be awaiting you.

Your lucky numbers this week: 26, 27, 29, 31.

24–30 JUNE 2000

No one and nothing can interfere with your plans for this week. This will be a delightful week, when you can do exactly as you please. Home and job pressures ought to be reduced considerably. Trips and visits will be successful, especially if you are visiting dear friends or relatives you have not seen for some time. They will be pleased to see you.

Your lucky numbers this week: 13, 14, 16, 30.

1 JULY–7 JULY 2000

Meet people halfway. Seek compromise solutions wherever possible. You will not get very far if you try to go it alone this week. This is the right time to think about the future. Pay attention to matters of security in old age. Invest in your own future, rather than splurging on things that won't last.

Your lucky numbers this week: 11, 28, 31, 32.

8–14 JULY 2000

An excellent period for all romantic matters. You are clearly able to let your partner know how you feel concerning just about any aspect of life, and you have more than enough nerve to accomplish a daring personal plan. When you need support, you should find that it is ready and waiting in the wrings. This is a period for action.

Your lucky numbers this week: 1, 11, 16, 26.

15–21 JULY 2000

This is another busy week, but do make certain that you know what is expected of you in advance. Nobody can really tell you how you should behave at the moment, even if that is exactly what most individuals seem to be doing. By the weekend a new attitude to an old problem can help you out no end.

Your lucky numbers this week: 10, 13, 25, 28.

22–28 JULY 2000

Do not be embarrassed about thinking big, because there is every chance that you can make your most grandiose schemes pay off this week. The reaction of people in your vicinity is extraordinary and leads you to believe that you can succeed with almost anything that occurs to you.

Your lucky numbers this week: 1, 16, 28, 30.

29 JULY–4 AUGUST 2000

Things are still looking good, though probably slowing down just a little as the weekend presents a break from work. Now you should turn your attention towards personal matters, which look more exciting than they have done for ages. Remove any obstacles from your personal path quickly.

Your lucky numbers this week: 3, 5, 11, 28.

5–11 AUGUST 2000

Some deep thinking provides new personal insights into all sorts of personal concerns. This does not prevent you from being yourself and from doing what comes naturally at work and socially. You might fancy a change of scene after work, and can probably spend some time with a person who is special.

Your lucky numbers this week: 15, 26, 28, 31.

12–18 AUGUST 2000

Family and domestic matters take up most of your time this week, leaving little room to work on your career prospects. Patience is required, but you might find this hard to discover within yourself at the moment. Experience and common sense count in most situations right now.

Your lucky numbers this week: 13, 21, 22, 33.

19–25 AUGUST 2000

The domestic sphere of life continues to take priority, and you may be planning to spend more time with your closest ones this week. In the meantime, you need to finish dealing with more practical matters in this period, so that you can pick up the baton next week in a positive way.

Your lucky numbers this week: 4, 11, 28, 31.

26 AUGUST–1 SEPTEMBER 2000

You should now have more time to spend on the more practical aspects of life and you can even turn rather difficult situations to your advantage. It is only a matter of time before you discover that a difficult problem is about to be solved, and you will be pleased to put on your thinking cap for the benefit of a friend.

Your lucky numbers this week: 2, 16, 28, 34.

2–8 SEPTEMBER 2000

The emphasis this week seems to be on pleasure, so there probably will not be enough time for practical considerations that this period might demand of you. Keep an eye on finances, which are probably not very strong at the moment. It will not be long before they improve at the end of the week.

Your lucky numbers this week: 1, 13, 25, 28.

9–15 SEPTEMBER 2000

Helpful and heart-warming news is on the way; it probably comes from a good friend abroad. The positive side of this is that you can take what is being said and use it as a platform for your own plans. Creating more space for yourself is also a part of the scenario in what should be a positive week.

Your lucky numbers this week: 1, 16, 28, 31.

16–22 SEPTEMBER 2000

Things are bound to slow down at the beginning of the week, but this is only short-term. You tend to have a shortage of both energy and time, so it would be sensible to find ways and means of using both rather carefully.

Your lucky numbers this week: 2, 6, 27, 30.

23–29 SEPTEMBER 2000

You can put invitations to good use now. It does not matter if the proposals come in business or are related to your social life – you cannot turn them down. Although it is still some time away, you may well have your sights firmly fixed on the summer period for next year and your hopes for it.

Your lucky numbers this week: 1, 13, 24, 25.

30 SEPTEMBER–6 OCTOBER 2000

With potentially exciting things occurring in all areas this week, there is nothing to prevent you from being cheerful and positive in your general approach. Not everyone is inclined to agree with you at present, but you possess the persuasive powers to bring almost anyone round to your point of view.

Your lucky numbers this week: 5, 6, 18, 29.

7–13 OCTOBER 2000

Professional and career projects bring certain pressures to bear that you could happily do without. Remaining calm and relaxed under most circumstances, however, you are likely to allow the slight irritations of the week to alter your perspective. Not everyone around you turns out to be equally helpful.

Your lucky numbers this week: 1, 3, 4, 20.

14–20 OCTOBER 2000

You need a greater capacity for self-expression. There are reasons to believe that this is what you discover this week. It is a time of sunshine and showers, no matter what the weather is really doing beyond the door. Even when slight difficulties do arise, you will have the capacity to deal with them in no time at all.

Your lucky numbers this week: 11, 13, 25, 30.

21–27 OCTOBER 2000

An excellent time for getting away from the major concerns of the world at large. This probably means that for once you become something of a hermit, which will certainly not suit everyone you come across. A slow and steady pace allows you to gradually get closer to something exciting waiting around the corner.

Your lucky numbers this week: 1, 4, 16, 27.

28 OCTOBER–3 NOVEMBER 2000

Co-operation is the keynote today. This is a splendid period for reaching agreement with your mate or partner on the best way to handle mutual affairs. It is a good time also to begin work on your home. Start those painting and redecorating jobs. Anything that gives you an opportunity to be artistic will have a special appeal. Speculation could be lucky for a change. This is a week for travel and dealing with distant affairs.

Your lucky numbers this week: 13, 27, 28, 31.

4–10 NOVEMBER 2000
If you can keep impulsive tendencies in check, this will be a good week for business. You must watch your extravagant streak. You may suddenly feel like laying out cash impulsively. Articles you are tempted to buy will be luxury items with little practical use. Worthwhile agreements can be consummated with people in superior positions. If you play your cards right, you could raise your earnings considerably in the not too distant future. People generally will be helpful and most sympathetic to your aims.

Your lucky numbers this week: 1, 12, 13, 27.

11–17 NOVEMBER 2000
Work will tend to be strenuous. You will have some difficulty keeping up your schedule this week. Nor will it be easy to promote teamwork. You must rely on yourself more than usual. You are good with words, but the gift of the gab may desert you. Health continues to require more attention. A week where you have to be cautious.

Your lucky numbers this week: 11, 21, 30, 32.

18–24 NOVEMBER 2000
No one and nothing can interfere with your plans for this week. This will be one of those enjoyable times when you may do exactly as you please. Home and job pressures ought to be reduced considerably. Get out and about more. If you feel you have been falling into a rut, take positive action to break the monotony. Trips and visits will be successful, especially if you are visiting friends or relatives you have not seen for some time.

Your lucky numbers this week: 1, 8, 19, 20.

25 NOVEMBER–1 DECEMBER 2000
Chances are that you will be feeling rather edgy this week. You will find it difficult to settle down to any job for very long. Members of your family will not help matters, with their additional demands and impulsive actions. Distant affairs continue to be rather confused. Sudden, unexpected events could disrupt plans for a journey in connection with your business interests.

Your lucky numbers this week: 15, 26, 30, 32.

2–8 DECEMBER 2000
Meet people halfway. Seek compromise solutions wherever possible. You will not get very far if you try to go it alone this

week. This is the right time to think about the future. Pay attention to matters connected with security in old age. Take out an insurance policy if you do not have one; otherwise think about whether you may need more coverage.

Your lucky numbers this week: 11, 13, 25, 26.

9–15 December 2000

This is the ideal week for travel and drumming up support in new areas. You will find it easy to get along with influential people you meet for the first time. If you are seeking a new position you may well be lucky and find just the job that is tailor-made for you.

Your lucky numbers this week: 6, 7, 9, 20.

16–22 December 2000

Keep out of the public eye. Secret agreements could pay off for you. It is important not to let too many people in on what you are currently negotiating. You can be inclined to gossip, but you must button your lip in order to protect your own interests. Trust no one with information that you have been asked not to share. The mail is important this week, and business correspondence should not be neglected.

Your lucky numbers this week: 1, 2, 16, 27.

23–29 December 2000

You could be in a fidgety mood during this rather slow, dull week. Do not act impulsively. Accept the fact that nothing of any great significance is going to happen. Rats who are housewives will feel cut off and isolated if stuck at home for any extended length of time. This is not a favourable week for dealing with influential people; wait for better opportunities.

Your lucky numbers this week: 1, 2, 4, 27.

30 December 2000–5 January 2001

People will be unco-operative. It will be difficult to fathom the reason why superiors are refusing to support your ideas. It may be rather boring, but it would be in your very best interests to deal solely with routine matters. It is unlikely that you will make any money from speculative ventures right now.

Your lucky numbers this week: 1, 16, 29, 33.

6–12 January 2001

Relatives will be overly sensitive. Be careful that your sharp tongue does not get you into trouble. What you say could easily be taken the wrong way by an older member of your family who has not been feeling well recently. Avoid emotional scenes at all costs. This is a good week for work requiring mental agility.

Your lucky numbers this week: 11, 27, 28, 30.

13–19 JANUARY 2001

Use your imagination. The best sort of work to concentrate on this week is something that gives you an opportunity to make full use of your natural artistic talent. Keep out of the way of superiors. Influential people will be awkward, unwilling to grant favours. Travel will not be fruitful if you are trying to drum up support.

Your lucky numbers this week: 2, 5, 18, 29.

20–26 JANUARY 2001 (24 JANUARY: CHINESE NEW YEAR – YEAR OF THE SNAKE)

Although you may visualize all sorts of idealistic concepts, you may be striving for what lies beyond the bounds of practicality. Home life needs to be handled with more common sense. Arguments within the household may be unavoidable as a prelude to sorting out your domestic problems. Even new plans now in the making are likely to dissolve completely.

Your lucky numbers this week: 11, 16, 28, 30.

THE SIGN OF THE
Ox

The Chinese name for the Ox: Niu
The second sign in the Chinese zodiac
The hours governed by the Ox: 1am–3am
The corresponding sign in the Western zodiac: Capricorn
Element: Water
The direction of the pole: Negative

*

The Year of the Ox in the Western Calendar

19 February 1901–7 February 1902 Metal Ox
6 February 1913–25 January 1914 Water Ox
25 February 1925–12 February 1926 Wood Ox
11 February 1937–30 January 1938 Fire Ox
29 January 1949–16 February 1950 Earth Ox
15 February 1961–4 February 1962 Metal Ox
3 February 1973–22 January 1974 Water Ox
20 February 1985–8 February 1986 Wood Ox
7 February 1997–27 January 1998 Fire Ox

Famous People Born Under the Sign of the Ox

Madeleine Albright, Hans Christian Andersen, Johann Sebastian Bach, Warren Beatty, Menachem Begin, Jon Bon Jovi, William Blake, Napoleon Bonaparte, Jeff Bridges, Willy Brandt, Richard Burton, Barbara Bush, King Juan Carlos of Spain, Barbara Cartland, Charlie Chaplin, Bill Cosby, Sammy Davis Jr, Princess Diana, Walt Disney, Dustin Hoffman, Anthony Hopkins, Saddam Hussein, Don Johnson, Jane Fonda, Gerald Ford, Adolf Hitler, Jack Lemmon, Heather Locklear, King Harald of Norway, Dustin Hoffman, Emperor Hirohito, Eddie Murphy, Benjamin Netanyahu, Jessica Lange, Jawaharlal Nehru, Paul Newman, Jack Nicholson, Robert Redford, Rod Steiger, Peter Sellers, Sissy Spacek, Bruce Springsteen, Meryl Streep, Margaret Thatcher, Tung Chee Wah, Twiggy, Vincent Van Gogh, Henning Hai Lee Yang (author).

The Ox in a Nutshell

POSITIVE QUALITIES
You are diligent, willing to learn, methodical, righteous, correct, faithful and very enduring.

NEGATIVE QUALITIES
You are stubborn, a bad loser, conservative and can be rather self-centred.

CAREER SUGGESTIONS
You will succeed as a good politician, general, farmer, engineer and in other professions where you can show your strong side as a leader.

Main Features of the Ox

You are diligent, positive and helpful. However, you tend to run your own show and can be rather stubborn and authoritarian. Some will find it difficult to work with you because you are tough and not always very co-operative.

LUCK

You appreciate the little things in life, but you are extremely proud to see that your work is giving results. You work hard and you are destined to succeed.

MONEY

You take care of what you have and build on your previous efforts. You can become very rich and famous through what you are doing; even something you learned as a child can bear fruit.

WORK

You are fond of teamwork when it is needed, but you can be rather manipulative. You like to work alone, and enjoy a senior role in order to have full control. You like to see and know what is going on around you.

SOCIAL LIFE

You get on well with the people you choose to deal with. You can be very shy and introverted when you find yourself among people you do not know well.

BUSINESS

You are sharp and observant, and always see possibilities around you. Because of your positive attitude and smart nature, you will make a lot of money.

LOVE

You are very romantic in nature, but you like to court the one you love and care for. You know how to make people take notice of you, and people appreciate your positive and stable nature.

PARENTS

Many Oxen find that their parents are not overly eager to engage themselves in their lives. The relationship might at times be rather strenuous and difficult.

SISTERS AND BROTHERS

You have a relatively good relationship with siblings, as long as they learn to observe your space and try not to be too dominant.

CHILDREN

You are fond of children and like to take responsibility. You may have many children, and they will love you dearly.

TRAVEL

You love travelling, and you are especially fond of the pure nature of the countryside. You like trees and greenery, and you never refuse the chance of exploring exotic sites and places you have never visited before.

HEALTH

You are strong and extremely robust, just like an Ox. Illness will keep away from you as you lead a healthy life, and you can look forward to good and prosperous later years.

INVESTMENTS

Your investments are well thought out and planned, and seldom give you problems. With your strict sense of business and power of consideration, your projects will make you very rich.

TALENTS

You are a hard worker. You are often not concerned whether you make money or not, as long as you have a chance to do your work well and run your own show. Life can be hard at times but because of your powers of endurance you will always pull through.

PROSPECTS

Life has much to offer, though you could display more love and affection to people around you. If you are not faced with new challenges, life will tend to be too boring for you.

What Kind of Ox Are You?

THE WOOD OX 1925, 1985

This is the good Ox from the continents of the world. You are enterprising and multi-talented and know exactly how to make use of your abilities. Life can be rather difficult at the beginning, but it will be easier when you grow older.

THE FIRE OX 1937, 1997

This is the Ox who lives near the rivers. You are both wise and brave. You can also be very authoritarian. At the beginning of your life you will have to work hard, but you will gain footholds step by step. The later stages of your life will be wonderful.

THE EARTH OX 1949, 2009

This is an Ox who stays happily at the farm, where there is a great deal of activity. You like to work hard. There will be no lack of possibilities and you know how to make use of your expertise. You are both artistic and very creative, which will be major assets in life.

THE METAL OX 1901, 1961

This is an Ox who is always on the go. You are very pleasant and also very enterprising. You like to care for people around you. At the beginning of your life, it seems rather tough, as you will work hard to make ends meet. But when you grow up, you know how to achieve things. You will have a happy life after all.

THE WATER OX 1913, 1973

This Ox stands within an enclosure. You are very lucky and your life is harmonious and safe. You will be very fortunate in finding a suitable partner, and you will be successful in making money. You manage well and you will have support from people around you. In other words – a very lucky Ox.

The Ascendants of the Ox

11PM–1AM: THE HOUR OF THE RAT 'ZI'

An Ox with a strong sentimental streak. The Rat's charm will soften you up and make you more flexible and communicative. However, you will never forget an insult. You also know how to keep your financial matters in order.

1AM–3AM: THE HOUR OF THE OX 'ZHOU'

You can be very militant and authoritarian. If someone steps a toe out of line, you will stamp on it. You are born with a strong sense of self-control and dedication. Unfortunately you lack humour and imagination. An Ox that no one should make fun of.

3AM–5AM: THE HOUR OF THE TIGER 'YIN'

An engaged and compelling Ox with a lively personality. You can never be shy or discreet, and you say what you mean. You are tough and rather bad-tempered, and people around you should be warned of your behaviour.

5AM–7AM: THE HOUR OF THE RABBIT 'MAO'

People will have difficulties in making you change your standpoint, but at least you are tactful and diplomatic – a rather pleasant Ox in other words. You appreciate art and prefer to have a relaxed manner in your daily work.

7AM–9AM: THE HOUR OF THE DRAGON 'ZHEN'

You will have strong support from others to get on with your work. It is a shame that you are not more flexible, otherwise you could advance in your career. Try to be more diplomatic and tactful, so the world will smile to you.

9AM–11AM: THE HOUR OF THE SNAKE 'SI'

This combination makes you a little shy and secretive, and also less receptive to the advice of others. You tend to be very conceited and stubborn, and enjoy being alone. Luckily, you are smart and know how to survive.

11AM–1PM: THE HOUR OF THE HORSE 'WU'

A very happy and satisfied Ox, with many positive aspects coming from the Horse. With the circus Horse in you, you love to dance. This Horse might distract you from achieving your previous goal: you should be careful.

1PM–3PM: THE HOUR OF THE GOAT 'WEI'

A very artistic Ox, with many gentle features. You are more understanding and receptive to others' views. You are also very business-minded and know how to make money from your talents.

3PM–5PM: THE HOUR OF THE MONKEY 'SHEN'

A cunning but funny Ox who does not take problems seriously. With the Monkey's influence, you will not need to dwell on such matters, as you always have an ace under your sleeve. You are a real winner.

5PM–7PM: THE HOUR OF THE ROOSTER 'YU'

You are energetic and responsible for your actions. You like to argue before doing anything. Often you apply your colourful rhetoric instead of your iron fists. This makes a good combination of both soldier and priest.

7pm–9pm: the Hour of the Dog 'Xu'

A serious fighter for justice could be rather boring if not saved by the Dog's stable temper. At least you are willing to listen to what others have to say before you put them on trial.

9pm–11pm: the Hour of the Pig 'Hai'

A pleasant, home-loving Ox, though you might be very demanding and conservative. You lack the confidence to do things thoroughly. Luckily, you are very diligent so this gives you some kind of compensation. You are also very fond of food and forget to keep yourself in shape.

The Year Ahead

No one who has ever watched a herd of Oxen moving calmly across an open plain can have failed to be impressed by their great natural majesty. When harnessed to the yoke, no other animal pulls a heavier load for such long hours.

With the ability to plough on against all opposition and to arouse confidence in those around him, seemingly by his very presence, the Ox has not surprisingly occupied more than a fair share of the world stage. Those born under this sign are destined for greatness and to make their mark as leaders of men. A conservative, the Ox despises novelties and gimmicks; the modern world is not for him. Trying to understand the Ox is a thankless and unproductive task. Any attempt to approach this most private of all creatures will only succeed in making him clam up. And the harder you try, the further he retreats. But because he is a born leader, any fears or uncertainties he encounters can never be admitted, either to himself or to others. As one might expect, the high-minded and ambitious Ox cannot bear to be thwarted, least of all by another Ox.

So people born under this sign are diligent and patient, home-loving and ambitious. You like to work hard and get to the top, step by step, and show great responsibility in whatever you do. Sometimes you seem to be very reserved and prefer to keep your thoughts to yourself. You will have a small circle of friends, but they will remain loyal to you. You are fond of quiet, cosy surroundings, and most of the time you seem to be calm and peaceful, unless you feel provoked. Then you can become a monster in your outrage. The most dangerous animals in the world are not Tigers or Lions, but wild Oxen.

Because of your great loyalty and punctuality you will enjoy success in whatever you do – on the condition that you are allowed to carry out your tasks by yourself. You will go far in politics or farming and in any field where expertise is vital. Furthermore, you could also be an artist, as you are born with creative talents in you. Your life will be interesting, but full of tasks to solve. The Ox born in spring will be very happy and have less to attend to than those born in summer and autumn. The winter Ox will also take it easy, but will have to watch out not to end up as steak on the dinner table.

You will meet challenges and surprises in the Year of the Dragon. With the right attitude, you will be able to confront any problems and even make the progress you are longing for. Your plans will proceed, though perhaps not at the desired speed. Unfortunately you will have to work hard in order to make ends meet, but you will meet influential people who will give you a helping hand. The last part of 2000 will be much better than the first part – something you can look forward to. A reward is not very far off.

Week By Week For People Born Under the Sign of the Ox

5–11 FEBRUARY 2000 (5 FEBRUARY: CHINESE NEW YEAR – YEAR OF THE DRAGON)

Pay as much attention as you can to creative work. Do not neglect your natural talents. It might be possible to make cash on the side and brush up on skills that have been neglected. Take up a hobby that once meant a great deal to you but has been over-looked because of pressure at work. In other words, a very creative week, where you have the chance to be constructive.

Your lucky numbers this week: 1, 11, 13, 25.

12–18 FEBRUARY 2000

Continue with your efforts to accomplish a creative feat. There should be no disturbing influences to slow you down. Money can be earned by paying more attention to hobbies and second jobs than from anything connected with your career. A very good week for contacting influential people.

Your lucky numbers this week: 3, 4, 5, 11.

19–25 FEBRUARY 2000

You are in the middle of a favourable period. Be sure that you make the best of the excellent opportunities presenting themselves to you now. This will be a fairly slow, quiet week, but good openings may lay the foundation for moves you wish to make in the near future.

Your lucky numbers this week: 1, 12, 20, 23.

26 FEBRUARY–3 MARCH 2000

You will find it easier to get along with members of your family. If you are married, you should be able to overcome differences with your spouse. Try to involve yourself in activities where your partner can take an active role; co-operation will bring you closer together. Trips will be enjoyable. This week is also outstanding for single Oxen. Romance will prevail more than it has for some time.

Your lucky numbers this week: 11, 13, 25, 30.

4–10 MARCH 2000

Go easy with money and think carefully before investing in anything that could jeopardize your resources. Risks are unlikely to pay off and creative projects must be kept in check. Do not advance your plans just because a superior has promised support verbally. Pull your head out of the clouds.

Your lucky numbers this week: 10, 12, 13, 25.

11–17 MARCH 2000

There will be good opportunities to express your point of view. Take advantage of the chance you have to address a large group of people whose support could be valuable. An excellent week for travel and for handling all matters pertaining to distant affairs. Your creative flair will be much in demand.

Your lucky numbers this week: 2, 11, 29, 30.

18–24 MARCH 2000

The health of a loved one could cause you concern. More of your spare time will have to be devoted to caring for others. Personal activities or a project you have been hoping to promote will have to be postponed. You will not find it easy to make any sacrifices at the end of the week.

Your lucky numbers this week: 1, 13, 25, 27.

25–31 MARCH 2000

You may be feeling a bit under the weather. Recent events have probably left you rather drained. It would be a good idea to pay attention to personal health matters, especially diet. No important business transaction should take place this week. Matters under discussion ought to be left until after you have some time to think things over.

Your lucky numbers this week: 3, 4, 15, 26.

1 APRIL–7 APRIL 2000

Control your temper. This week you are inclined to jump to conclusions too quickly, which could be damaging for your career, especially if you deal with business people. Allow more give and take to enter into your professional relationships. Otherwise, the week is good for romantic experiences.

Your lucky numbers this week: 1, 13, 24, 31.

8–14 APRIL 2000

Your mind will be on matters taking place far away. You may have to do some travelling. Certainly it will be difficult to ignore events taking place elsewhere. Useful agreements can be consummated. Do not hold out for exorbitant terms; you could lose a good contract if you price yourself out of the market.

Your lucky numbers this week: 1, 13, 25, 28.

15–21 APRIL 2000

Be prepared for a slow, uneventful week. As long as you can adapt to the steady pace, you will have no problems. If you try to force things, however, you will probably wear yourself out without achieving anything of real value. Turn your attention to health problems; with the business scene rather quiet, this is a ideal time to pay attention to minor ailments.

Your lucky numbers this week: 11, 29, 30, 32.

22–28 APRIL 2000

Be ready for anything. It may be difficult to stick to the schedule you have worked out for this week. Loved ones will be unpredictable; their extra demands could make you miss an important appointment in the middle of the week. Business matters have to be taken seriously.

Your lucky numbers this week: 11, 13, 25, 29.

29 APRIL–5 MAY 2000

Let someone else take centre stage. This will be a period to look, listen and learn. What you learn is likely to be interesting, and it is possible to pick up a great deal from someone else's performance. Influential people will be impressed by your calm manner: show you can keep your head while others around you are losing theirs. Do not allow yourself to be pressured into signing any documents.

Your lucky numbers this week: 1, 2, 11, 13.

6–12 MAY 2000

Be first; beat your competitors to the punch and get off to an early start. This will be a good week for those who immerse themselves totally in work. Relatives will be congenial. If there are problems to cope with at home, you should find that an older family member is willing to stand in for you.

Your lucky numbers this week: 3, 24, 25, 30.

13–19 MAY 2000

Peaceful conditions should make it possible to deal with work requiring intense concentration. It would be silly to waste your time attempting to launch anything new. Projects you have in mind need far more work before they can be suggested to people who could offer valuable support. Take one step at a time: you will succeed.

Your lucky numbers this week: 2, 4, 21, 25.

20–26 MAY 2000

Use this week to smooth out the differences that recently arose between you and your boss. Your charm will help you to work out better terms with people you will undoubtedly have to rely upon in one way or another. This will be a good weekend to build up your relationship with influential people around you.

Your lucky numbers this week: 11, 13, 27, 34.

27 MAY–2 JUNE 2000

If you can keep impulsive tendencies in check, this will be a good week for business. If you play your cards right, your earnings will soon increase. People will be helpful and sympathetic to your aims.

Your lucky numbers this week: 6, 11, 13, 29.

3–9 JUNE 2000

So long as you keep spending on pleasurable activities to a minimum, this can be a quite satisfactory week. One word of warning: do not buy off people you feel could help you out. Paying for expensive lunches and dinners in ritzy clubs will not bring what you want in your career. Influential people will be more co-operative if they see you are prepared to pull your full weight.

Your lucky numbers this week: 11, 13, 24, 26.

10–16 JUNE 2000

The tone of your close relationships will begin to improve. It will be much easier for you to talk to members of your family. If you are married you stand a better chance of bringing your spouse round to your point of view. Travel to far-off places is indicated. Whatever you do, you will be rewarded.

Your lucky numbers this week: 1, 18, 29, 32.

17–23 JUNE 2000

Meet people halfway. Seek compromise solutions wherever possible. You will not get very far if you try to go it alone this week. This is the right time to think about the future. Pay attention to matters concerning security in old age. Invest in your own future, rather than splurging on things that won't last.

Your lucky numbers this week: 2, 3, 14, 26.

24–30 JUNE 2000

An excellent time for any romantic matter for the Ox. You can clearly let your partner know how you feel concerning just about any aspect of life, and you have more than enough nerve to accomplish a daring personal project. When you need support, you should find that it is ready and waiting in the wings. This is a period for action.

Your lucky numbers this week: 16, 27, 28, 30.

1 JULY–7 JULY 2000

This is another busy week, but make certain that you know what is expected of you in advance. Nobody can really tell you how you should behave at the moment, even if that is exactly what most individuals seem to be doing. By the weekend a new attitude to an old problem can help you out no end.

Your lucky numbers this week: 1, 12, 23, 34.

8–14 JULY 2000
Do not shirk from thinking big, because there is every chance that you can make your most grandiose schemes pay off this week. The reaction of people is extraordinary, making you believe that you can get away with almost anything that you think of.

Your lucky numbers this week: 3, 16, 28, 36.

15–21 JULY 2000
Things still look good, though they are probably slowing down just a little as the weekend brings a halt to matters in your practical life. Now you should make plans about personal concerns, which look more exciting than they have done for a long time. Remove any obstacles from your personal path in haste.

Your lucky numbers this week: 11, 22, 24, 35.

22–28 JULY 2000
Deep thought brings new insights into all sorts of personal matters. This does not prevent you from being yourself or from doing what comes naturally in business and socially. You might fancy a change of scene after work and can probably spend some time with a special person.

Your lucky numbers this week: 6, 11, 16, 27.

29 JULY–4 AUGUST 2000
Family and domestic matters take up most of your time this week, leaving little time to create the practical space you need to advance your career. Some patience is required, but you might find it hard to discover this within yourself just for the moment. Experience and practical common sense count in most situations right now.

Your lucky numbers this week: 1, 12, 33, 34.

5–11 AUGUST 2000
The domestic sphere of life continues to take up much of your time and you may be planning to spend more time with your nearest and dearest. Meanwhile you need to tidy up practical

matters in this period, so that you can pick up things again next week in a positive way.

Your lucky numbers this week: 3, 6, 12, 36.

12–18 AUGUST 2000

You should this week have more time to spend upon the practical aspects of life and you can even turn rather difficult situations to your own advantage. It is only a matter of time before you discover that a difficult problem is about to be solved and you will be pleased to put your mind to work for the benefit of a friend.

Your lucky numbers this week: 1, 11, 16, 33.

19–25 AUGUST 2000

The emphasis this week seems to be placed on pleasure, so it sees unlikely that there will be enough time to deal with practical considerations that this period might demand of you. Keep an eye on finances, which are probably not very strong at the moment. It will not be long before they improve at the end of the week.

Your lucky numbers this week: 12, 23, 24, 30.

26 AUGUST–1 SEPTEMBER 2000

Helpful and heart-warming news is on the way, and it probably comes from a good friend abroad. You can take what is being said and use it as a platform for your own plans. Creating more space for yourself is also part of the scenario in what should be a positive week.

Your lucky numbers this week: 1, 2, 16, 28.

2–8 SEPTEMBER 2000

Thing are bound to slow down a little bit for the beginning of the week, but this is only short-lived. You tend to lack both time and energy, so it would be sensible to find ways and means of using both rather carefully.

Your lucky numbers this week: 11, 29, 31, 33.

9–15 SEPTEMBER 2000

You can put invitations to good use now. It does not matter if the proposals come in business or are related to socializing: you cannot turn them down as you stand to gain from them. Although summer has just said farewell, you will have lots of good ideas for making the most of the summer months next year. A trip abroad is indicated.

Your lucky numbers this week: 6, 13, 16, 27.

16–22 SEPTEMBER 2000

With potentially exciting things happening in all areas of life, there is nothing to prevent you from being cheerful and positive in your general approach. Although some people disagree with you at present, you possess the persuasive powers to bring almost anyone round to your point of view this week.

Your lucky numbers this week: 1, 2, 4, 15.

23–29 SEPTEMBER 2000

Professional and career projects bring certain pressures to bear that you would rather do without. As you are calm and relaxed in most situations, however, you are likely to allow the slight irritations of the week to bring new perspectives. Not everyone around you turns out to be equally helpful.

Your lucky numbers this week: 1, 16, 28, 31.

30 SEPTEMBER–6 OCTOBER 2000

You need a greater capacity for self-expression and you are likely to learn this now. It is a time of sunshine and showers, regardless of the weather outdoors. But even when slight difficulties do arise, you can handle them in no time at all.

Your lucky numbers this week: 8, 18, 24, 34.

7–13 OCTOBER 2000

An excellent time for turning away from the major concerns of the world at large. This probably means that for once you become something of a hermit, which will certainly not suit everyone you come across at present. A gradual pace gets you closer to something exciting around the corner.

Your lucky numbers this week: 9, 12, 33, 35.

14–20 OCTOBER 2000

Co-operation is the keynote today. This is a splendid period for working out an agreement with your partner on the best way to handle mutual affairs. It is also a good time to begin work on your home. Start those painting and redecorating jobs. Anything that gives you an opportunity to be artistic will have special appeal. Speculation could be blessed with luck for a change. This is a week for travel and dealing with distant affairs.

Your lucky numbers this week: 1, 16, 27, 30.

21–27 OCTOBER 2000

If you can keep impulsive tendencies in check, this will be a good week for business. You must watch your extravagant streak. You may suddenly feel like spending cash wildly. Items you are tempted to buy will be luxuries that have little practical use. Worthwhile agreements can be consummated with people in superior positions, and if you play your cards right, you could raise your earnings considerably in the not too distant future. People will generally be helpful and sympathetic to your aims.

Your lucky numbers this week: 6, 23, 29, 30.

28 OCTOBER–3 NOVEMBER 2000

The sort of work that you can carry out could easily lead to promotion. You will find that people remain very co-operative. This is the right week to show your qualities of leadership. Your intuition should be accurate and reliable and there is no reason why you should take a wrong step. The week will be successful because you know what you do.

Your lucky numbers this week: 16, 27, 29, 31.

4–10 NOVEMBER 2000

The Ox is in the middle of a generally rewarding period. Be sure that you make the best of the excellent opportunities presenting themselves to you now, as this will be a busy and interesting week where you see openings for laying the groundwork for future prospects.

Your lucky numbers this week: 12, 23, 28, 30.

11–17 NOVEMBER 2000

Apparently you are suddenly having a tough time. You could be rocked by what is taking place in business circles now. Work is probably strenuous. You are going to be hard pressed to maintain your busy schedule. Luckily you are strong, and ultimately you will manage.

Your lucky numbers this week: 1, 15, 16, 24.

18–24 NOVEMBER 2000

Now you must keep calm. Do not resort to panic measures regarding recent events. Pull yourself up by your bootstraps.

Your vivid imagination could be making more of what is, after all, only a minor setback to your plans. Close associates will be most helpful; colleagues will do all that they can to reassure you.

Your lucky numbers this week: 4, 15, 26, 30.

25 NOVEMBER–1 DECEMBER 2000

This week will be similar to last week. You are lacking in confidence when you have no real cause to be self-effacing. Home life will be complicated. Arguments could break out with loved ones, probably because you are in such a tense frame of mind. It will be difficult to keep up with pressing business.

Your lucky numbers this week: 1, 2, 6, 20.

2–8 DECEMBER 2000

Control your temper. You are inclined to jump to conclusions too quickly. This tendency may be harmful for your career, especially if you are working with business people. Your partner or another family member may be worried about money and may not wish to be honest about how extravagant they have been recently. No important plans should be put into action at this time.

Your lucky numbers this week: 3, 13, 25, 29.

9–15 DECEMBER 2000

Self-reliance is required. This is one of those difficult weeks when the Ox cannot win support for projects just when it is most needed. In many ways you will be torn down the middle. The conflict of loyalties between responsibility to your family and a sense of loyalty to the firm for which you work will be extremely difficult to handle. Now you need to be diplomatic and flexible.

Your lucky numbers this week: 1, 5, 11, 16.

16–22 DECEMBER 2000

Keep things familiar. This is not a week for setting out on a journey. Deal with people you know you can trust. It would be better to add finishing touches to work already in hand than to attempt to launch a new project. The week will be romantic and interesting for love-related matters.

Your lucky numbers this week: 1, 2, 16, 28.

23–29 DECEMBER 2000

There may be a new romance in the air this week, but you will have to grasp the opportunity. If, however, you are already attached, it would be wise to handle these matters delicately. Although you seem to be rather extravagant these days, your finances seem to allow for it. This week is good for enjoying yourself with your loved ones.

Your lucky numbers this week: 1, 6, 10, 11.

30 DECEMBER 2000–5 JANUARY 2001

You must try not to hurry routine matters. Errors made now could prove costly at a later date. Hobbies will give you some break. This is a pleasant week for anything that gives free rein to the artistic side of your nature.

Your lucky numbers this week: 3, 8, 18, 26.

6–12 JANUARY 2001

Nothing of any particular importance is likely to occur. Make no difficulties for yourself, and use this easy-going period to unwind. You will not be troubled by other people's problems. There will be good opportunities to think about your own future: consider your career goals to make sure you have not lost touch with your true aims and aspirations.

Your lucky numbers this week: 1, 8, 18, 34.

13–19 JANUARY 2001

Money problems should ease off. A letter or a telephone call will have a reassuring effect. This is a quiet week, offering opportunities to amend recent mistakes. You will certainly find it easier to deal with authority figures. Even your boss will show greater willingness to understand your personal problems.

Your lucky numbers this week: 3, 4, 18, 29.

20–26 JANUARY 2001

Although you are good at saving, occasionally you may be overcome with a desire to splash out. This is one of those weeks. Boredom may give you a craving for unusual entertainment, but be wary of travelling too far afield for your pleasure. A week of thrills.

Your lucky numbers this week: 8, 18, 24, 31.

THE SIGN OF THE
Tiger

The Chinese name for the Tiger: Hu
The third sign in the Chinese zodiac
The hours governed by the Tiger: 3am–5am
The corresponding sign in the Western zodiac: Sagittarius
Element: Wood
The direction of the pole: Positive

*

The Year of the Tiger in the Western Calendar

8 February 1902–28 January 1903 Water Tiger
26 January 1914–13 February 1915 Wood Tiger
13 February 1926–1 February 1927 Fire Tiger
31 January 1938–18 February 1939 Earth Tiger
17 February 1950–5 February 1951 Metal Tiger
5 February 1962–24 January 1963 Water Tiger
23 January 1974–10 February 1975 Wood Tiger
9 February 1986–28 January 1987 Fire Tiger
28 January 1998–15 February 1999 Earth Tiger

Famous People Born Under the Sign of the Tiger

Kofi Annan, Princess Anne, Sir David Attenborough, Queen Beatrix of the Netherlands, Ludwig van Beethoven, Tom Berenger, Agatha Christie, Tom Cruise, Leonardo DiCaprio, Emily Dickinson, Isadora Duncan, Queen Elizabeth II, Roberta Flack, Fredrick Forsyth, Jodie Foster, Charles de Gaulle, Sir Alec Guinness, Dwight D. Eisenhower, Hugh Hefner, William Hurt, Aleksandr Lebed, Charles Lindbergh, Karl Marx, Marilyn Monroe, Demi Moore, Rudolf Nureyev, Marco Polo, Beatrix Potter, Diana Rigg, Lionel Ritchie, Kenny Rogers, Mark Spitz, David Steel, Dylan Thomas, H.G. Wells, Stevie Wonder, St Francis Xavier, Frank Yang (the author's father), Natalie Wood.

The Tiger in a Nutshell

POSITIVE QUALITIES
You are strong, brave, honest, imaginative, ambitious and have good leadership qualities.

NEGATIVE QUALITIES
You are restless, impulsive, rebellious, stubborn, aggressive and difficult to work with.

CAREER SUGGESTIONS
You are a born leader and can handle any situation dealing with administration and leadership. Otherwise you could be a good private eye or police inspector, as you can see through people. You love travelling and meeting people, so jobs dealing with media will be of great interest to you.

Main Features of the Tiger

You are forceful and energetic, but tend to be very ruthless at times. You should slow down for your own sake, and try to take one step at a time. Otherwise you are a great leader, with many interesting qualities.

LUCK

You will have much luck in your life, but you may exaggerate more than is good for you. If you take on risky projects without footholds, you might lose everything you have gained and have to start your life all over again.

MONEY

You will be very rich and powerful if you manage to steer clear of too many uncertain projects. You will either be very rich and famous, or remain very anonymous throughout your life.

WORK

You are of course a great leader, but your style might be a little bit too tough and unconventional for some people around you.

SOCIAL LIFE

You are active and love entertaining others. You have a magical power over your loved ones.

BUSINESS

You may make money in a very unconventional way. This might mean that you may either run a great business empire, or operate a criminal business, trying to avoid attention from the police.

LOVE

You are very romantic and enjoy the thrill of the chase. You will never be satisfied with whoever you have just managed to hunt down. To settle down with someone is not your style: you like to have several options at once.

PARENTS

Your parents do not quite understand you, so you might have trouble with them. It is wise to take care of them anyway, but it is best to do things that do not upset them.

SISTERS AND BROTHERS

You like to run your own show and do not bother to listen to your close ones. Relationships can be successful at times, but as you are so self-interested you may just try to avoid them.

CHILDREN

You think that having your own children is a marvellous idea, but it is quite certain that you will not have much time for them at all. You will have to think twice before conceiving children.

TRAVEL

You are very adventurous. Travelling is a must for you. The world's most famous travellers and adventurers are often born in the Year of the Tiger.

HEALTH

You are solid and strong, though you might overestimate your own power and position.

INVESTMENTS

You will make a lot of money, and you also might lose it all if you are too greedy. Try to stay on the line of the 'Golden Way', trading carefully with stocks and shares.

TALENTS

You are brave and strong, suited to any work in which you can show your strength. However, sometimes you get so carried away you risk running into trouble with the law. Pause to look before you leap.

PROSPECTS

You do a good job and are very detailed. You are the leader type, with great skills in management. Life can go up and down, and yours is never dull.

What Kind of Tiger Are You?

THE WOOD TIGER 1914, 1974

This is the resting Tiger; you are both self-confident and brave, and know what you want. Life brings you into contact with all kinds of people willing to support you. You can be both rich and powerful, but you will have to learn the art of diplomacy.

THE FIRE TIGER 1926, 1986

This is the Tiger who lives in the mountains. You are very curious, and tend to accumulate vast knowledge. You are very enterprising, perhaps even a bit restless and impulsive. You often need the ballast in order to get things done. To start you might think things are working too slowly, but by the end you will have worked things out.

THE EARTH TIGER 1938, 1998

This is the Tiger on the move. You are strong, even authoritarian, and like to do things your own way. You prefer to listen to yourself than the advice of others. You will have a wonderful and exciting life, but take care with the many traps around you.

THE METAL TIGER 1950, 2010

This is the Tiger who comes down from the mountains. A restless and impulsive person, you are also tolerant and show great generosity to people around you. You are a master of gathering people around you, and you are a great leader who knows how to use your power and position.

THE WATER TIGER 1902, 1962

This is the Tiger from the deepest woods. You are both strong and impulsive. Somewhat self-sacrificing and too honest for your own good, life can seem like a constant struggle, but you will manage to fight back and survive your problems.

The Ascendants of the Tiger

11PM–1AM: THE HOUR OF THE RAT 'ZI'

A tough guy who loves nature. At the same time you like quarrelling for the sake of it and later on ask for pardon. Luckily you are not revengeful and not the sort to bear grudges. The Rat in you gives you a good economic sense, because you are fond of counting your money.

1AM–3AM: THE HOUR OF THE OX 'ZHOU'

You are strong-willed and bad-tempered. Maybe the Ox in you will give you more discipline, so that you need not get off the hook so fast. You can be a quiet, nice guy after all.

3AM–5AM: THE HOUR OF THE TIGER 'YIN'

You have all the teeth and the claws required, and you are a person who is brave and prefers to move straightforwardly. Rather unconventional is your nature, and you like to make use of your hunting instincts too. If someone is looking for an interesting companion, you will be the right choice.

5AM–7AM: THE HOUR OF THE RABBIT 'MAO'

You have a delicate nature. The Rabbit in you makes you less impulsive, with the result that you are smart enough to make the right decision to keep yourself out of trouble.

7AM–9AM: THE HOUR OF THE DRAGON 'ZHEN'

You are very ambitious, aiming at progressing in your career all the time. The Dragon in you will strengthen your ego and you can be a very good leader if you stop mistrusting other people.

9AM–11AM: THE HOUR OF THE SNAKE 'SI'

Maybe the Snake in you will teach you to be quiet. The Snake will also bring you great advantages, keeping you calm and self-controlled, so the Tiger will not lose its head during negotiations.

11AM–1PM: THE HOUR OF THE HORSE 'WU'

The Horse in you is more practical. At the same time it also advises you not to get involved in any risky projects. This combination could create some problems, as both of the signs are very fond of their freedom and at times tend to forget their responsibilities.

1PM–3PM: THE HOUR OF THE GOAT 'WEI'

You are quiet and observant, but you are also extremely jealous and possessive. The Goat in you makes you interested in fine art and the good side of the life, so you will be more social and active in cultural activities. The temper of the Tiger will be slowed down in such a nice combination.

3PM–5PM: THE HOUR OF THE MONKEY 'SHEN'

Here the force of muscle meets intelligence. Let us hope they come together in the right proportions. This combination can take you far in life. You are brave and have foresight.

5PM–7PM: THE HOUR OF THE ROOSTER 'YU'

You possess a fascinating personality, someone who wants to quarrel and fight meeting someone who is a trouble-shooter. You will not allow anyone to get away with anything unless you are being heard – and they will probably have no other choice.

7PM–9PM: THE HOUR OF THE DOG 'XU'

You are a very reasonable and co-operative Tiger, resulting from the influence of the Dog. Your bad temper will be slowed down by the Dog's willingness to compromise, but your mouth is just as sharp as a shaving blade.

You are very impulsive and naïve. Contented and satisfied – as long as you get what you want. Though many people find you hard work and possessive, this results from your desire to get attention and friendship from people around you.

The Year Ahead

The Tiger is famous for its strength and determination. No beast on earth combines the same degree of beauty, strength and energy. Add bravery, and you complete the list of enviable attributes given to those born in the Year of the Tiger. Physically and mentally, you are not without your opponents. Although you may win many a fight, the battle is a very different story. In any setting, the Tiger is not one to go unnoticed. You are a dynamic revolutionary who will not stand by while others are given a raw deal. And nobody should ever try to push you around. You like a fight, and few are better equipped to come out on top. As the Tiger you are both impetuous and idealistic, and are quick to find faults in others. You react outspokenly against authority of every kind, especially when you see it as corrupt. You are the natural ringleader – just think of Karl Marx and his influence on the greatest revolutions in history.

As the Tiger, you will take on any job that gives you a chance to show your courage and imagination. You are very careful of your own reputation, and like to run the show and be in the centre of attention. You are good at selling yourself and getting the right publicity, not just for your own sake, but also for what you represent.

Tiger women are very active and funny. You like to dress up for parties and are fantastic hostesses at any events you arrange. Furthermore, you are good mothers, though you might be a little too strict. In any case you are good at raising your children so that they will not lack anything in life.

The Tiger has many good qualities. You are brave and honest, and radiate energy, so people usually notice you. If you can build your patience, you can go far and live a good and satisfactory life.

This year will be very exciting for you. Many opportunities await the Tiger in 2000 and throughout the year you would do well to act boldly and with determination. Over the year, the Tiger will see many chances that will present new and interesting opportunities that you can turn to your advantage. A longer trip is also awaiting you, and if you get the opportunity to travel to a far-off location, accept the invitation. You will need to pay attention to your travel documents before you embark on the trip.

Week By Week For People Born Under the Sign of the Tiger

5–11 FEBRUARY 2000 (5 FEBRUARY: CHINESE NEW YEAR – YEAR OF THE DRAGON)

This is going to be an exciting year for the Tiger. The sort of work that you have the chance to do could easily lead to promotion. You will find that people remain very co-operative. This the right week to show your qualities of leadership. If you trust your intuition, you should do no wrong. The week will be successful because you know what you do.

Your lucky numbers this week: 8, 17, 24, 35.

12–18 FEBRUARY 2000

Routine matters should take priority. This easy-going week gives you the opportunity to tackle ordinary jobs that were recently postponed. You will be able to catch up with – if not get ahead of – your schedule. The week is also good for romantic events. Try to do something on your own. It would be pointless to try to do business. Do not bother influential people with your creative projects. You could lose the support of someone who has been extremely helpful in the past if you pester them in their week of peace and rest.

Your lucky numbers this week: 4, 5, 6, 17.

19–25 FEBRUARY 2000

You are very sensitive this week and you might feel that you lack the opportunities you need to show off your skills at work. However, if you try to do so, you might fall out with your colleagues. Apply your tact and you will manage to handle matters very successfully after all. The last part of the week is very favourable.

Your lucky numbers this week: 4, 19, 21, 31.

26 FEBRUARY–3 MARCH 2000

This week reminds you very much of last week, except where love and romance are concerned. There will be some quarrels between you and your chosen one and it will be up to you to sort it out, especially as you have a roving eye at the moment. But this flirtatious behaviour will not make you popular, so stop it or you will get yourself into stormy waters.

Your lucky numbers this week: 1, 18, 21, 28.

4–10 MARCH 2000

Your luck will change. People you are in touch with will be congenial. You should feel on top of situations. More time can be given to improving your health, so relax and unwind your frayed nerves. Even your partner might think you are tense – slow down and enjoy life.

Your lucky numbers this week: 14, 18, 28, 34.

11–17 MARCH 2000

Do not be a fool with money. Considering how you need to save at the moment, it would be extremely unwise to lend money to friends. Try to avoid cash transactions in close relationships. People who borrow money and promise to pay it back within a specified period may not be able to do so, which could cause bad feelings.

Your lucky numbers this week: 15, 26, 28, 31.

18–24 MARCH 2000

Catch up with any work left over from last week. Bring your finances up-to-date. With nothing new to divert your attention, you can use this week to sort out your affairs. Assess all correspondence relating to tax and insurance; be sure that you claim all the benefits that are yours by right.

Your lucky numbers this week: 8, 18, 24, 30.

25–31 MARCH 2000

You will find it rather difficult to get into full swing at your place of work. There are likely to be a few problems to sort out before you can move into action. Colleagues will not be inclined to fall in with your ideas and you will have to seek new ways to get things done.

Your lucky numbers this week: 4, 12, 14, 31.

1 APRIL–7 APRIL 2000

Little will take place to create discord and you may have more time on your hands than usual. Do not spend too much on entertainment. Spare time should be devoted to any hobby or pastime that helps to improve your mind. Do what you can to increase your knowledge of subjects that have always been of particular interest to you.

Your lucky numbers this week: 3, 18, 24, 26.

8–14 APRIL 2000

You are in the middle of a generally rewarding period. Be sure to make the best of excellent opportunities presenting themselves to you now. This will be a hectic and interesting week where you see openings that lay the groundwork for future prospects.

Your lucky numbers this week: 8, 14, 24, 31.

15–21 APRIL 2000

It seems that you will be having a hard time, all of a sudden. You could be shaken by what is taking place in business circles now. Work is apt to be strenuous and you are going to be pushed to keep up with your busy schedule. Luckily you are strong, and you will be able to manage.

Your lucky numbers this week: 3, 16, 24, 36.

22–28 APRIL 2000

You will have to remain calm. Do not resort to panic measures in response to recent happenings, and pull yourself up by your bootstraps. Your vivid imagination could be making more of what is, after all, only a minor setback. Close associates will be most helpful; colleagues will do all that they can to reassure you.

Your lucky numbers this week: 2, 8, 24, 35.

29 APRIL–5 MAY 2000

This week will be similar to last week. You lack confidence when in fact you have no real cause to be self-effacing. Home life will be complicated. Arguments could break out with loved ones, probably because you are in such a high-strung mood. It will be difficult to keep on top of pressing business.

Your lucky numbers this week: 5, 18, 24, 36.

6–12 MAY 2000

Control your temper. You are inclined to jump to conclusions too quickly and this could be damaging for your career, especially if you are weighing up business people. Your partner or another family member may be worried about money and may not wish to tell you how extravagant they have been recently. No important plans should be implemented at this time.

Your lucky numbers this week: 1, 8, 11, 23, 32.

13–19 MAY 2000

Your luck will change. People you come into contact with will be congenial and you should feel on top of situations. More time can be devoted to improving your health. Relax, and unwind your frayed nerves. Even your partner might think you are tense: slow down and enjoy life.

Your lucky numbers this week: 4, 18, 24, 36.

20–26 MAY 2000

Do not be foolish with money. As you need to save at the moment, it would be extremely unwise to lend money to friends. Try to avoid cash transactions in close relationships. People who borrow money and promise to pay it back within a specified period may not be able to do so, which could cause bad blood.

Your lucky numbers this week: 8, 18, 24, 31.

27 MAY–2 JUNE 2000

Catch up with any work left over from last week. Bring financial affairs up-to-date. With nothing new to divert your attention, you can use this week to sort out your interests. Go over all correspondence relating to tax and insurance; be sure that you claim all the benefits that are yours by right.

Your lucky numbers this week: 9, 18, 22, 36.

3–9 JUNE 2000

You will find it rather difficult to get into full swing at your place of work. There are likely to be a few problems to deal with before you can get into action. Colleagues will not be inclined to fall in with your ideas, so you will have to seek new ways to get things down.

Your lucky numbers this week: 8, 11, 24, 32.

10–16 JUNE 2000

Little will take place to create discord and you may have more time on your hands than usual. Do not spend too much on entertainment. Spare time should be devoted to any hobby or pastime that helps improve your mind. Do what you can to increase your knowledge of subjects that have always been of particular interest to you. Friends will offer pleasant company.

Your lucky numbers this week: 1, 18, 24, 33.

17–23 JUNE 2000

Wishy-washy impulses, a feeling of inadequacy, vague doubts and fears that have no sound foundation: these are handicaps from which Tigers may suffer this week. Influential people may be difficult to please, but this is no reason to worry about your own performance on the job.

Your lucky numbers this week: 4, 12, 24, 32.

24–30 JUNE 2000

Face up to what has to be done boldly. Do not try to wriggle out of your responsibilities. Throw yourself into your job. There is no way to solve your financial problems through gambling. Once you come to grips with what is bothering you, coping with it will not be that difficult.

Your lucky numbers this week: 1, 18, 23, 35.

1 JULY–7 JULY 2000

Home continues to be most important. Your activities will centre around loved ones. Do what you can to satisfy people who mean a great deal to you. Recent differences with your partner can be settled amicably with a little give and take on both sides. Efforts to improve your home or property are sure to increase its value.

Your lucky numbers this week: 4, 8, 24, 36.

8–14 JULY 2000

Do not ask for special favours. You will not find influential people willing to grant an increase in salary, promote you or allow you to leave work earlier than usual. Disagreements will occur if you try to press your demands. Accept the current situation. Home will be the best place for you this week.

Your lucky numbers this week: 1, 18, 23, 34.

15–21 JULY 2000

Do all you can to bring happiness into the lives of loved ones. It will give you great pleasure to put a smile on the face of your partner or child. You will certainly earn great satisfaction from giving. Entertainment will be easy to find and is unlikely to cause any extraordinary expense.

Your lucky numbers this week: 1, 15, 24, 32.

22–28 JULY 2000

People at a distance from you will continue to be extremely cooperative. You will find it easier to deal with strangers than with regular business contacts. The new and the untried will be a stimulus and routine concerns will be rather difficult to concentrate on. This is not a good week for dealing with authority figures. Wait before discussing your future career prospects.

Your lucky numbers this week: 8, 18, 27, 36.

29 JULY –4 AUGUST 2000

An element of deception is operating this week. Someone at your place of employment may be out to hoodwink you for one reason or another. Everything that you are told in connection with your business should be checked out. It may be that a colleague wants you to make a fool of yourself in the eyes of a superior. A certain amount of jealousy is at play.

Your lucky numbers this week: 8, 18, 24, 30.

5–11 AUGUST 2000

You are probably not thinking straight. This is the wrong week to play hunches or make snap decisions. Speculative propositions should be avoided, and gambling could be disastrous. Take special care when travelling this week.

Your lucky numbers this week: 1, 16, 24, 31.

12–18 AUGUST 2000

Probably the best week this month, if not of the year. Tigers will be extremely aware of everything that is going around them and their intuition will be exceptionally sharp. There will be a good opportunity to show your worth to people who matter. It may be possible to leapfrog over competitors into a job that you have been keen to take on. Even romance is starred. Single or married, you will be happy in the company of that special person in your life.

Your lucky numbers this week: 8, 15, 24, 32.

19–25 AUGUST 2000

Influential people will sit up and take notice of your words. You have a greater chance than usual to win the support of superiors. Agreements made now will allow you to make steady progress with a creative project, though routine work is unlikely to progress quite so smoothly this week.

Your lucky numbers this week: 1, 8, 12, 30.

26 AUGUST–1 SEPTEMBER 2000

This will be a slow and boring week. Your great danger could be boredom. If you find yourself at a loose end, try to get involved in something productive. An excess of spare time could lead you to seek extravagant pleasure. There may be differences of opinion at home. Those who are dating a new person must be careful not to be too aggressive.

Your lucky numbers this week: 1, 3, 30, 32.

2–8 SEPTEMBER 2000

One of the best weeks of the month for home and family affairs. An about turn by loved ones means that you can make steady progress with jobs you are keen to tackle at home. Health problems can be sorted out and you should be feeling in much better shape physically.

Your lucky numbers this week: 2, 11, 18, 26.

9–15 SEPTEMBER 2000

This week can be used for catching up with tasks you have neglected. Though you have had a fairly busy time last week, you will still have to sort out things that have been left behind. Romance will contain no problems this week either. Your love life may not be very exciting, but you will be grateful for the security of your present relationship.

Your lucky numbers this week: 2, 18, 24, 31.

16–22 SEPTEMBER 2000

Unexpected income could come your way. Do what you can to make money from a creative enterprise. Hobbies could easily develop into part-time jobs. See what you can do to win support for your new ideas from people in positions to help you. Romance will be exciting and stimulating this week.

Your lucky numbers this week: 13, 14, 30, 31.

23–29 SEPTEMBER 2000

A useful week for contacting people who are often hard to see. Influential colleagues may be able to put you in touch with someone who can be of special benefit to your career. It would be best not to fix rigid a timetable this week.

Your lucky numbers this week: 16, 18, 24, 36.

30 SEPTEMBER–6 OCTOBER 2000

No pressure will be placed on you now. You will respond well to the added responsibility of finding your own pace at which to work. Superiors will be too busy to listen to the new ideas that you are keen to promote. It would be best to stick to routine matters for now.

Your lucky numbers this week: 8, 18, 24, 34.

7–13 OCTOBER 2000

Matters at work are extremely sensitive. You will find that colleagues do not see eye-to-eye with you now. Try as you might, it will be practically impossible to get your ideas accepted by them. No changes in work patterns should be attempted. Do not make any impulsive decisions about love affairs.

Your lucky numbers this week: 9, 10, 24, 31.

14–20 OCTOBER 2000

Those involved in any kind of legal proceedings will encounter satisfactory results this week. However, be careful to stay on the right side of the law, since you may become involved again. This weekend favours all those connected with arts and the entertainment business.

Your lucky numbers this week: 8, 10, 22, 36.

21–27 OCTOBER 2000

A week of good news. Expect financial rewards for work done in the past. Your mail will also prove to be of importance, so do not throw anything away until you have read it thoroughly. The weekend is a good time for romance. Younger members of the sign will find parents restrictive and unco-operative.

Your lucky numbers this week: 2, 18, 24, 31.

28 OCTOBER–3 NOVEMBER 2000

Pay attention to matters of domestic importance that you have been ignoring all week. Now is the time to settle things on the home front. If partners have been unco-operative, you should find them less so this week. Romance is likely this weekend.

Your lucky numbers this week: 1, 18, 24, 32.

4–10 NOVEMBER 2000

This week will be marked by a lack of activity. There is unlikely to be much friction, which will certainly come as a welcome relief. Your partner will agree with most of your ideas for this week. It looks as if you may be spending more time at home than usual. Pay attention to older relatives.

Your lucky numbers this week: 2, 18, 21, 36.

11–17 NOVEMBER 2000

Confusion early in the week could slow you down. Do not put too much faith in promises made by associates. Colleagues are likely to be unpredictable, and promises made verbally may be conveniently forgotten. Push ahead with creative enterprises.

Your lucky numbers this week: 8, 12, 24, 33.

18–24 NOVEMBER 2000

A lack of energy could make this a rather slow period. You will have some difficulty getting into top gear this week, and money matters need to be approached with caution. You cannot afford extravagant impulses. The problems of loved ones could put you to unavoidable expense this week.

Your lucky numbers this week: 3, 18, 24, 31.

25 NOVEMBER–1 DECEMBER 2000

Another difficult week ahead. In the areas of romance and finance you have to be extremely cautious. Be on guard at all times and take no situation for granted. One false move now could upset plans carefully laid for the future.

Your lucky numbers this week: 9, 10, 24, 34.

2–8 DECEMBER 2000

You would not have to battle very hard for what you want this week, so it is an excellent time to ask favours of superiors. Try to refrain from requests for financial help; these can come later. This weekend a member of the opposite sex will be of particular help.

Your lucky numbers this week: 18, 24, 27, 30.

9–15 DECEMBER 2000

Whatever is happening in your working surroundings will affect you later this week, so try to keep abreast of what is going on. Colleagues are evasive and unco-operative, so you will have to do your own investigating. Domestic problems interfere with entertainment this weekend.

Your lucky numbers this week: 8, 12, 24, 27.

16–22 DECEMBER 2000

Imagination and intuition can be turned to good use this week. Any creative ideas you have at present should be written down for future reference. Those involved in creative jobs should have an excellent week full of original ideas. Hunches should be acted upon and new notions tried out.

Your lucky numbers this week: 3, 18, 24, 36.

23–29 DECEMBER 2000

You continue to be the most appealing person around, which is why others express their love for you in no uncertain terms. Even this could get you down after a while, particularly since a part of you feels like a hearty argument this week! You might be disappointed in this respect.

Your lucky numbers this week: 12, 18, 24, 30.

30 DECEMBER 2000–5 JANUARY 2001

Romance goes through a specially rocky time this week. Permanent partnerships will also meet problems. If you are suddenly attracted to a member of the opposite sex, make certain that you can follow up on initial feelings. This is not a time to put relationships in jeopardy.

Your lucky numbers this week: 8, 14, 23, 31.

6–12 JANUARY 2001

A work week that drags slowly by. Routine seems to be unnecessarily difficult and you are thwarted by interfering colleagues.

Try not to lose your temper as you will come out the worse for wear if you become involved in arguments. Confrontations with marriage partners should also be avoided.

Your lucky numbers this week: 1, 2, 8, 24.

13–19 JANUARY 2001

A week full of tensions, not helped by pressures of work. Your workload will be higher than normal and you will find yourself struggling towards the end of the week. This weekend should be spent in the company of people who relax and humour you.

Your lucky numbers this week: 1, 4, 5, 30.

20–26 JANUARY 2001 (24 JANUARY: CHINESE NEW YEAR – YEAR OF THE SNAKE)

Avoid wasting time and energy this week, as you will need all your strength for a potentially exhausting business trip. Don't be afraid to go off the beaten track and get things done. Your boss will appreciate your aggressive attitude in pulling in a new contract.

Your lucky numbers this week: 13, 15, 16, 30.

THE SIGN OF THE
Rabbit

The Chinese name for the Rabbit: Tu
The fourth sign in the Chinese zodiac
The hours governed by the Rabbit: 5am–7am
The corresponding sign in the Western zodiac: Scorpio
Element: Wood
The direction of the pole: Negative

*

The Year of the Rabbit in the Western Calendar

29 January 1903–15 February 1904 Water Rabbit
14 February 1915–2 February 1916 Wood Rabbit
2 February 1927–22 January 1928 Fire Rabbit
19 February 1939–7 February 1940 Earth Rabbit
6 February 1951–26 January 1952 Metal Rabbit
25 January 1963–12 February 1964 Water Rabbit
11 February 1975–30 January 1976 Wood Rabbit
29 January 1987–16 February 1988 Fire Rabbit
16 February 1999–4 February 2000 Earth Rabbit

Famous People Born Under the Sign of the Rabbit

Prince Albert, Idi Amin, Harry Belafonte, Ingrid Bergman, King Bhumibol, Lewis Carroll, Fidel Castro, John Cleese, Confucius, Marie Curie, Moshe Dayan, Albert Einstein, Peter Falk, Peter Fonda, James Fox, David Frost, Cary Grant, Oliver Hardy, Bob Hope, Whitney Houston, John Hurt, Michael Keaton, John Keats, Julian Lennon, Arthur Miller, Walter Mondale, Roger Moore, Tatum O'Neal, Christina Onassis, George Orwell, Eva Peron, Neil Simon, Jane Seymour, Dusty Springfield, Sting, Josef Stalin, Leon Trotsky, Queen Victoria, Orson Welles, Norman Wisdom, Willie Yang.

The Rabbit in a Nutshell

POSITIVE QUALITIES
Intelligent, observant, cultivated, peaceful, friendly, romantic and very loyal to your loved ones.

NEGATIVE QUALITIES
Worried, cowardly, pedantic and self-occupied.

CAREER SUGGESTIONS
You can be a good diplomat, teacher, artist or priest and not the least a good administrator in any kind of business.

Main Features of the Rabbit

You are quiet, positive and always very charming. However, you can be so self-interested that you might be a little absent at times. Many people will find you very special. Sometimes you find it difficult to communicate.

LUCK
You are fond of peace and like quiet places. Quarrels and disagreements will disturb your life and make you very depressed.

MONEY
You are dependent on others' support in order to get by. But if you find someone who understands you and is willing to

support you, then you can make great money from your creativity.

WORK

You are fond of people and can be very shy. You prefer solitude and inner peace and you will thrive if you can work by yourself in your own quiet manner.

SOCIAL LIFE

If you live a sheltered life, you will just get along fine. But should you be brave enough for nightlife, you will actually discover that you like meeting different people after all. Influential friends will flock around you.

BUSINESS

You are sharp and intuitive, and see possibilities more easily than most people around you. Even when you least expect it, you will become very rich.

LOVE

You are very romantic and sentimental, always willing to serve the one you have chosen as partner. You know the arts of seduction and flirtation, and you are always well dressed. If you dare to enter deeper waters, then you may find the right partner, since you are extremely charming.

PARENTS

You will have loveable and harmonious parents, though they can be rather demanding, because they love you so dearly.

SISTERS AND BROTHERS

You have a good and solid relationship with siblings, as there is much love and understanding between you.

CHILDREN

You are very fond of children, but find them quite a responsibility. The Rabbit can bring many children into the world, because you are really fond of sex.

TRAVEL

You love travelling and exploring other countries' customs and lifestyles. You are very fond of exotic food and drinks. It would be extra nice to spend the time together with your partner right beside you.

HEALTH

Usually you have a very delicate body that needs a lot of attention and nursing. Take good care of yourself and try to avoid unnecessary sickness.

INVESTMENTS

With your strong intuition you will have to be a master at making money. You will have luck with your investments; if you can keep a level head, you will be able to save a fortune.

TALENTS

You are intelligent and observant, and can do very well in business. If you make proper use of your charm and tact you will be able to go far in life.

PROSPECTS

You will live a happy life, because you are good at paying attention to people around you. Your life is never dull, and you take every day as a new challenge.

What Kind of Rabbit Are You?

THE WOOD RABBIT 1915, 1975

This is the spiritual Rabbit. You will develop powerful religious beliefs. You will also find yourself a good and resourceful partner and need not worry about your future. You manage well on your own, and receive much support from people around you.

THE FIRE RABBIT 1927, 1987

This is the wise and thinking Rabbit who makes his demands known. You are enterprising and clever and manage to conduct your affairs in an outstanding way. Your life is harmonious and comfortable, and your old age will be safe and without problems.

THE EARTH RABBIT 1939, 1999

This is the Rabbit from the deepest woods, a Rabbit who is smart and clever. At the beginning of your youth you will have some problems with your life. But when you get older, everything will work out right for you. You can become both rich and famous.

THE METAL RABBIT 1951, 2011

This is the Rabbit who is looking at the moon. There are a lot of activities and plans, and you are good at exploiting the possibilities.

You will have great powers when you get older. In the later stages of your life, you will enjoy a happy old age.

THE WATER RABBIT 1903, 1963

This is the Rabbit who stays in the mountains. You are good at making people notice you. You will have a happy life with your family, and your old age will be smooth and comfortable.

The Ascendants of the Rabbit

11PM–1AM: THE HOUR OF THE RAT 'ZI'

You are smart, loveable and well informed. The Rat in you will make you more lively and demanding. In other words, a Rabbit who is very smart and willing to compromise.

1AM–3AM: THE HOUR OF THE OX 'ZHOU'

The influence of the Ox makes you more independent and self-assured than any other type of Rabbit. You can reckon on great success with the strength and self-control of the Ox. You are bound to go far in life with such a good combination.

3AM–5AM: THE HOUR OF THE TIGER 'YIN'

You are a fast thinker. The Tiger in you makes you more aggressive than usual, but fortunately enough the Rabbit has overall control.

5AM–7AM: THE HOUR OF THE RABBIT 'MAO'

You are the peace-loving type, a person who never takes sides with anybody, because you want to be nice to everyone. You are very diplomatic, of course. One thing is for sure: you are loved by everyone around you.

7AM–9AM: THE HOUR OF THE DRAGON 'ZHEN'

You are tough and ambitious, and you like to do things by yourself. You would prefer to control others in order to carry out your well-made plans. In other words, you are a very enterprising and cunning little Rabbit.

9AM–11AM: THE HOUR OF THE SNAKE 'SI'

You are very insecure and tend to be very thoughtful though rather conceited at times. You do not take any advice from others. Furthermore, you are very sensitive and governed only by your own intuition and emotions.

11AM–1PM: THE HOUR OF THE HORSE 'WU'

A very happy and adventurous Rabbit who enjoys the self-esteem of the Horse. You can make good use of these two signs, because both offer you the chance of advancing in life and competing with others.

1PM–3PM: THE HOUR OF THE GOAT 'WEI'

The Goat in you makes you more sympathetic and generous. The result of this combination make you more tolerant and friendly, but unfortunately you will tend to spend more money than you acquire. Try to be careful with your money.

3PM–5PM THE HOUR OF THE MONKEY 'SHEN'

A cunning and provocative Rabbit. Your intuition and icy nature will be covered up by the mischief of the Monkey. People around you will have to expect unexpected surprises from you, because you are very crafty.

5PM–7PM: THE HOUR OF THE ROOSTER 'YU'

You possess a fascinating personality. Here is someone who wants to quarrel and fight meeting someone who is a troubleshooter. You will not allow anyone to run away with anything unless you are being heard – and the others will probably have no choice in the matter.

7PM–9PM: THE HOUR OF THE DOG 'XU'

The Rabbit becomes more open and friendly because of the influence of the Dog. You will be less self-occupied and care more for others less fortunate than yourself. You are a very honest and comfortable Rabbit, with many admirers around you.

9PM–11PM: THE HOUR OF THE PIG 'HAI'

A solitary animal who is slightly unsettled, but perfectly organized. You act rather mysteriously; one never knows what you are really up to. You are friendly, though, and when it is needed you can even be very helpful.

The Year Ahead

When you are born under the sign of the Rabbit, you are born under the sign of virtue. Blessed with an inner mystery that many find both frightening and bewitching, Rabbits have included great personalities such as Trotsky and George Orwell and perhaps the greatest physicist of all time, Albert Einstein.

You are very sensitive and circumspect in your dealings with everyone you meet, and possess an overpowering need to be surrounded by a passive and agreeable environment, giving you the best possible credentials for any position that requires diplomacy. As the Rabbit, you listen carefully when spoken to and can remember in detail any conversation or polite argument. With your open ear and readiness to sit quietly, you make a superb diplomat, and your objective judgement can be a great asset should you choose to take up the legal profession.

You hate unnecessary quarrels. Outside your home and family, confronted with any subject, you try to settle things down in a peaceful manner. If you are the boss, an angry and upsetting scene is the last thing you want. As the Rabbit you have a natural flair for business and will make a name for yourself if you avoid too much competition. Your social ease and good manners make you an ideal partner, and these are invaluable assets when dealing with people at any level. For all your great skill in sniffing out a bargain, the Rabbit does not have an original mind, so you will have to ally yourself with someone with imagination and business expertise.

Rabbit women have neat, often artistic handwriting. You spend a lot of time on your often extremely beautiful hair. Most of you let it grow long, especially if it is dark, and many of you prefer to live alone than marry for the sake of it, though without a man to fuss over you may become a little melancholic. In any circumstances, you are friendly and caring, and you do everything in your power to make your nearest and dearest enjoy your parties. However, you are not good at applying your full energies, because you like to do too many things at one time.

In China the Rabbit is associated with luck and fortune, and luckily you will always manage to get things done with little effort. You are a quick thinker and talented, and if you can put the work before pleasure, then you can go far in life. You will have many good friends, and your life will never be dull.

This will be a wonderful year for you. Finally talk about promotion and financial success will bear fruit. You can reckon on great opportunities and success during the year, which can make up for the losses of earlier periods of your life. Favourable messages from your close circle of friends represent positive experiences for you and your loved ones. There will also be an increase in new members of your family during this very good period.

Week By Week For People Born Under the Sign of the Rabbit

5–11 FEBRUARY 2000 (5 FEBRUARY: CHINESE NEW YEAR – YEAR OF THE DRAGON)

The year will start in a very calm manner. This rather restful week will come as a welcome break. Slow down; you allow your nerves to get rather wound up at times. There will be nothing to interfere with your regular duties. Do not try to start anything new. Conditions will be far too quiet to develop new ideas. Rabbits who have been suffering from minor ailments should be able to get satisfactory treatment now.

Your lucky numbers this week: 8, 18, 24, 35.

12–18 FEBRUARY 2000

Your most important work is likely to be accomplished mid-week. Differences with loved ones can be smoothed out; this bears well for the whole week. People with whom you come in contact will be lacking energy. Pleasure and entertainment are unlikely to have much appeal. No important changes in the way finances are handled should be attempted.

Your lucky numbers this week: 8, 31, 32, 33.

19–25 FEBRUARY 2000

Restraint is vital in all matters connected with money. Pay small bills and check your bank statement. Try to discover exactly how your savings stand. Do what you can to explain the situation to the more extravagant members of your family. This week is not a time when any of your brood can afford to go on a spending spree.

Your lucky numbers this week: 1, 18, 24, 36.

26 FEBRUARY–3 MARCH 2000

This week will rush by. There will be a number of items to deal with in faraway places. Deal with these in person; this will be more effective than trying to sort out issues by telephone or letters. The personal touch is needed now. Useful information can be obtained to enable you to advance your creative enterprises.

Your lucky numbers this week: 11, 13, 24, 30.

4–10 MARCH 2000

Conditions continue to favour Rabbits. Creative projects have a good chance of developing. This is not a good week, however, for borrowing or lending money. Friends may press you to give a helping hand. If you do get involved with other people's problems, try to be businesslike about being paid back. In this way you will safeguard your own interests and probably save your friendship from being totally ruined.

Your lucky numbers this week: 1, 8, 24, 32.

11–17 MARCH 2000

You should end this week pleased with your progress. There will have probably been some awkward moments, but you have the ability to cope with difficult people and situations with great style. Conditions favour you devoting as much time as you can spare to creative projects. This week should be pleasant and family members will be co-operative.

Your lucky numbers this week: 3, 4, 5, 17.

18–24 MARCH 2000

Unforeseen opposition from a loved one has to be handled sensitively. Do not be selfish and be sure that you devote a fair amount of time to members of your family. Much can be done around the house to increase its value. This is not a good week for travel. Short trips are favoured, rather than long journeys.

Your lucky numbers this week: 1, 8, 14, 23.

25–31 MARCH 2000

This is not a good week to try to drum up support for new projects. It will be easy to concentrate on paperwork. Use your time to bring the books up-to-date. Be sure that you have paid all bills and get your financial situation into some semblance of order.

Your lucky numbers this week: 1, 8, 24, 32.

1 APRIL–7 APRIL 2000

This will not be a busy week. You will probably have more time to yourself than is usual for a working week. Do not sit around doing nothing. There are many jobs that you can complete around the house and creative projects can be advanced a step ahead. Romance will have a special place in your life.

Your lucky numbers this week: 2, 18, 21, 33.

8–14 APRIL 2000

Another rather slow week. Because you feel restless it may be taxing to keep extravagant impulses in check. Keep your spending within reasonable limits. Do not splash out a large sum on a hobby that you have only recently taken up; you may soon get bored with it. It is wise to keep future security firmly in mind, so that money can be saved.

Your lucky numbers this week: 5, 6, 20, 30.

15–21 APRIL 2000

There will be opportunities to prove yourself at your place of employment. The best way to catch the eye of your boss is by showing that you are industrious and can knuckle down to a job. There is much that you can do to dispel doubts about your reliability. Prove that you can grit your teeth and keep up to schedule.

Your lucky numbers this week: 1, 4, 17, 20.

22–28 APRIL 2000

An erratic week. You will be more dependent on others than usual. There are likely to be delays because of late arrivals at the office or factory. No matter how much your colleagues irritated you, try not to lose your temper. Associates will be impulsive. Do not rely on people keeping promises made verbally.

Your lucky numbers this week: 8, 18, 24, 33.

29 APRIL–5 MAY 2000

A pleasant week for you and yours. Problems that have been in the back of your mind will be easier to deal with. Have a frank conversation with your beloved. Explain what has been worrying you. It would be best to bring differences out into the open and clear the air now. Chances are that you will be drawn more closely to your partner again. Creative work will become important this week.

Your lucky numbers this week: 1, 8, 24, 36.

6–12 MAY 2000

Some uncertainty will make this week rather difficult. You will not be able to agree with your partner or parent on the way to spend leisure time this period. Your ideas are unlikely to be acceptable to members of your family. Once you reach a compromise, it should be possible to enjoy holiday activities.

Your lucky numbers this week: 11, 18, 23, 30.

13–19 MAY 2000

This week will be marked by lack of activity. Nothing of any significance will take place, nor should you attempt to make anything gel. Deal with a backlog of work that has piled up. There are minor chores that you have been avoiding; this week affords a good chance to put your affairs in order.

Your lucky numbers this week: 1, 11, 24, 32.

20–26 MAY 2000

Nothing is likely to run according to plan. It would be best not to make too many important appointments as people will not be very reliable. Before setting off on a journey, check to be sure that the people you want to see have not forgotten the engagement. If you are careful, things will work out right for you.

Your lucky numbers this week: 14, 18, 23, 31.

27 MAY–2 JUNE 2000

Continue to be extremely careful about your financial situation this week. Leave nothing to chance as far as cash is concerned. Investments made now are unlikely to bring in anticipated returns. This is not a time to look for easy ways to make quick money.

Your lucky numbers this week: 18, 19, 24, 32.

3–9 JUNE 2000

Remain close to familiar surroundings. You will not achieve much if you attempt to drum up support for your ideas in other places. Rabbits who earn a living through buying and selling may find earnings dropping considerably, especially if most of their income comes through commission. Relatives will be difficult. Try to avoid arguments that lead nowhere.

Your lucky numbers this week: 8, 11, 20, 22.

10–16 JUNE 2000

Throughout the week you can get into top gear. Problems that are weighing you down will seem rather insignificant. The reason for your change of attitude is likely to be connected with excellent news about future career prospects. Your confidence will receive a boost from an unexpected source. Useful agreements can be consummated.

Your lucky numbers this week: 1, 2, 18, 19.

17–23 JUNE 2000

People will be attracted to your lively wit and enigmatic personality, and now you will find that you get even more attention. Your romantic partners will enjoy themselves more than they thought possible. Concentrate on personal matters. Careerwise, everything should be in good shape this week.

Your lucky numbers this week: 1, 18, 19, 23.

24–30 JUNE 2000

This week favours manual tasks. All those of you born under this sign who have to exert physical energy in your work should be able to increase your earnings. You should feel rested. Jobs that usually take a long time can be completed satisfactorily at record speed. This is also an optimum period for concluding private business deals.

Your lucky numbers this week: 1, 2, 3, 18.

1 JULY–7 JULY 2000

This week may be very unsettling for both single and married Rabbits. Partnerships will show signs of being less secure than you imagined. The business part of your life is also likely to be more delicate than ever. Assessing the overall situation, it appears unwise to take any impulsive actions this week.

Your lucky numbers this week: 1, 12, 13, 30.

8–14 JULY 2000

Early squabbles about money may have to be sorted out. Arguments with friends over cash are likely. There may be some difference of opinion concerning a recent debt. The amount is apt to be small, however, so it should not cause any lasting bad feeling. This will otherwise be an uneventful week.

Your lucky numbers this week: 2, 3, 13, 36.

15–21 JULY 2000

Do not embark on a long journey. Delay travel plans if at all possible. This is not a good week for dealing with people you do not know well. Health problems may require special attention.

Your lucky numbers this week: 12, 13, 33, 34.

22–28 July 2000
This will be a quiet and peaceful week – it might even seem a bit boring, depending on your taste. However, although you possess good insight, you might be a bit erratic in your behaviour towards your partner and those around you. Try to share your worries and your joys with those who really love you, and you will discover what love and friendship really mean.

Your lucky numbers this week: 3, 17, 29, 31.

29 July–4 August 2000
Unpredictable people could play havoc with your plans. An outing you have long been anticipating may have to be postponed at the last moment because of your partner's unpredictability. This will be a difficult week for personal relationships.

Your lucky numbers this week: 2, 12, 15, 36.

5–11 August 2000
You have a great chance of success in areas where you have failed in the past. Do all that you can to fulfil your personal desires and plans. Where romance is concerned, be much more bold. Take the initiative!

Your lucky numbers this week: 1, 11, 13, 31.

12–18 August 2000
Even though there will be good opportunities to advance your career at your place of employment, this will not be a happy or a memorable week. Problems connected with your home and family will be uppermost in your mind. Creative projects will be rather disappointing from a financial standpoint.

Your lucky numbers this week: 3, 12, 13, 33.

19–25 August 2000
Examine new ways of solving the problems of loved ones. You should be able to allocate time to seek knowledge that would help ease worries regarding home and family. Older relatives may offer some good advice. It is a week for listening to people who have more experience than you.

Your lucky numbers this week: 1, 15, 19, 32.

26 August–1 September 2000
Your quick-thinking mind could help beat competitors to the punch. It is a case of the early bird catching the worm. The worm

in question is likely to be a promotion that leads to better working conditions and pay. The co-operation that you receive from loved ones will enable you to put domestic worries out of mind and concentrate on essentials.

Your lucky numbers this week: 2, 12, 13, 33.

2–8 SEPTEMBER 2000

Do not offer to help people when you have a great deal scheduled. And do not rely too much on the integrity of others, for this could lead to being let down. Romantic matters will be disappointing. Someone you have secretly admired may make it clear to you in no uncertain terms that they are not interested in more than friendship.

Your lucky numbers this week: 9, 12, 13, 31.

9–15 SEPTEMBER 2000

Although rich in resourcefulness, you are sometimes poorly equipped to be doggedly persistent. This week you can let your imagination have full rein by all means, but also be practical when it comes to assessing relative values – especially financial ones. Any work tackled at home will add to the worth of your property. Try to handle DIY jobs yourself, rather than calling in a handyman.

Your lucky numbers this week: 9, 12, 20, 31.

16–22 SEPTEMBER 2000

This is not a week to let the emotional side of your nature have the upper hand. Problems connected with loved ones must be put to the back of your mind. There is little that you can do now to directly alleviate the worries that are confronting relatives. Purely practical matters must take precedence.

Your lucky numbers this week: 13, 14, 25, 36.

23–29 SEPTEMBER 2000

So long as you avoid gambling in any way, shape, or form, you should be reasonably pleased with events taking place. You feel as if a great burden has been lifted from your shoulders. Your partner will now be able to cope far better with their own responsibilities.

Your lucky numbers this week: 3, 14, 35, 36.

30 SEPTEMBER–6 OCTOBER 2000

This is a good time to spend more on your business in order to step up profits. Invest in whatever will save time and labour. Do not leave cash that could be put to good use in the bank. Regular work contains no unexpected problems. Romantic experiences are focused during this week.

Your lucky numbers this week: 1, 12, 13, 30.

7–13 OCTOBER 2000

Safety regulations must be observed. This is one of those weeks when accidents could occur if you do not keep your mind on the job at hand. Machinery must be operated with special care. Do not allow chatty associates to distract your attention. Travel could also be rather hazardous this week.

Your lucky numbers this week: 8, 12, 14, 31.

14–20 OCTOBER 2000

You may have been having some trouble sorting out relationships. The balance can be restored now. This is an excellent period for finding the same wavelength as your partner. You will find that loved ones are prepared to see your point of view.

Your lucky numbers this week: 1, 2, 5, 10.

21–27 OCTOBER 2000

Do not take anything or anyone for granted. You will find relatives rather unpredictable. Your partner may not wish to go through with agreed-upon plans for this week. Even though you previously asked their opinions and made the arrangements, you may find that your beloved is not willing to go along with your plans for pleasure and entertainment.

Your lucky numbers this week: 12, 15, 23, 33.

28 OCTOBER–3 NOVEMBER 2000

Co-operation is needed at your place of employment. Those Rabbits who feel that a salary increase is long overdue must not ask for a raise by themselves. Unity is important. Find people with jobs like your own, earning similar wages. You have a greater chance of having your request granted if you can speak with more than one voice.

Your lucky numbers this week: 4, 12, 13, 35.

4–10 NOVEMBER 2000

Take care as you handle money. Do not allow recent success to go to your head, and stick to your present lifestyle. There will be a desire to act like a big shot. Do not throw your money around trying to make good impressions.

Your lucky numbers this week: 1, 11, 13, 31.

11–17 NOVEMBER 2000

As long as you are not aiming too high, this can be a reasonably successful week. Ample time should be devoted to dealing with financial affairs. Those of you who require co-operation from others in order to carry out your work satisfactorily should try to improve the atmosphere at work.

Your lucky numbers this week: 10, 12, 13, 33.

18–24 NOVEMBER 2000

Travel will achieve good results. You will probably feel like a change of environment this week, and will be grateful for any opportunity to meet new people. Routine concerns will have little appeal now. You will be keen to get on with exciting new plans.

Your lucky numbers this week: 1, 12, 13, 31.

25 NOVEMBER–1 DECEMBER 2000

Do not devote too much time to run-of-the-mill jobs. It is important to allow the creative side of your nature more freedom. Be creative. Do not stifle your natural talents. Affairs in distant places continue to be quite lucrative.

Your lucky numbers this week: 9, 10, 16, 36.

2–8 DECEMBER 2000

All in all, this will be a fairly slow and uneventful week from the business angle. It may be a bit frustrating to have to leave a deal unfinished over the weekend. It would be extremely unwise to be too pushy. You could lose a valuable contact if you try to force things now.

Your lucky numbers this week: 1, 12, 13, 31.

9–15 DECEMBER 2000

As far as business goes, you should be on the ball. You will start this week in fine form, and have no problems when it comes to dealing with business colleagues. Your power of intuition should be good. The week is food for romantic matters.

Your lucky numbers this week: 1, 11, 34, 36.

16–22 DECEMBER 2000

Your personal life should be pleasant. There is plenty to keep you on the go but no more than you can deal with satisfactorily. Stand up for a friend, but only do so after careful thought, else you might cause problems for yourself further down the line. Documents need to be checked before you sign them.

Your lucky numbers this week: 16, 27, 28, 30.

23–29 DECEMBER 2000

Do not overestimate your influence this week, else you could come unstuck. You have the ability to be pompous on occasions, which might not go down that well with certain other people you have to deal with. A balance is important, however, since you do not want to earn credibility by looking humble.

Your lucky numbers this week: 1, 4, 27, 30.

30 DECEMBER 2000–5 JANUARY 2001

Personal matters could seem to be unsettled, which is unsatisfactory for you. Trapped inside yourself more than would normally be the case, you probably need someone with whom you can communicate on a deep level. Seek such people out; life will help by offering a fair selection.

Your lucky numbers this week: 9, 12, 13, 32.

6–12 JANUARY 2001

Home is the best place to be for all Rabbits. It is where your mind might choose to stay, even if your body must be somewhere else. You have the ability at present to inhabit a number of different realities, and this suits you down to the ground. Creative potential may not seem all that strong, but it should soon improve.

Your lucky numbers this week: 11, 12, 19, 23.

13–19 JANUARY 2001

Steadily, happily and successfully, you approach achievements that you never really expected this year. The fun thing about this week is that you have no idea what is going to happen next, but you can be fairly sure that most of it is going to please you. If you are feeling flush, this would be an ideal week for a number of shopping trips.

Your lucky numbers this week: 2, 3, 25, 26.

20–26 JANUARY 2001 (24 JANUARY:
CHINESE NEW YEAR – YEAR OF THE SNAKE)

Something in your life needs to be in better shape, so you become a sculptor of life this week, chiselling and scraping until you finally get what you want in the art gallery of your life. There is a problem here, however. By next week many of your ideas will have changed altogether – but that is art, is it not?

Your lucky numbers this week: 1, 12, 13, 31.

THE SIGN OF THE

Dragon

The Chinese name for the Dragon: Lung
The fifth sign in the Chinese zodiac
The hours governed by the Dragon: 7am–9am
The corresponding sign in the Western zodiac: Libra
Element: Wood
The direction of the pole: Positive

*

The Year of the Dragon in the Western Calendar

16 February 1904–3 February 1905 Wood Dragon
3 February 1916–22 February 1917 Fire Dragon
23 January 1928–9 February 1929 Earth Dragon
8 February 1940–26 January 1941 Metal Dragon
27 January 1952–13 February 1953 Water Dragon
13 February 1964–1 February 1965 Wood Dragon
31 January 1976–17 February 1977 Fire Dragon
17 February 1988–5 February 1989 Earth Dragon
5 February 2000–23 January 2001 Metal Dragon

Famous People Born Under the Sign of the Dragon

Princess Alexandra of Denmark, Joan of Arc, Jeffrey Archer, Joan Baez, Michael Barrymore, Count Basie, Julie Christie, James Coburn, King Constantine, Bing Crosby, Salvador Dali, Charles Darwin, Deng Xiaoping, Neil Diamond, Matt Dillon, Christian Dior, Placido Domingo, Kirk Douglas, Michael Douglas, Marlene Dietrich, Prince Edward, Sigmund Freud, Che Guevara, Edward Heath, Tom Jones, Martin Luther King, John Lennon, Abraham Lincoln, François Mitterrand, Ronaldo Nazario de Lima, Friedrich Nietzsche, Florence Nightingale, Nick Nolte, Al Pacino, Elaine Page, Gregory Peck, Pelé, Cliff Richard, Haile Selassie, Martin Sheen, Ringo Starr, Princess Stephanie of Monaco, Karlheinz Stockhausen, Shirley Temple, Andy Warhol.

The Dragon in a Nutshell

POSITIVE QUALITIES
Effective, intelligent, ambitious, honest, imaginative, elegant and proud.

NEGATIVE QUALITIES
Impatient, impulsive, demanding, prickly and self-centred.

CAREER SUGGESTIONS
Film star, entrepreneur, instructor, politician and any kind of work dealing with leadership.

Main Features of the Dragon

You are charming, positive and enterprising, but you have the tendency of running your own show and can be very demanding and authoritarian. Others will find you a little too tough and at times very difficult to work with.

LUCK
You are fond of the small joys of life, but you are also very keen on achieving status and power.

94

MONEY

You are very good at making money, and you are clever and smart so that whatever you touch becomes gold. When you learn to take one step at a time, you will certainly become very rich and famous.

WORK

You enjoy being with others, but you can be very manipulative when it suits you. Though you do not like to stay alone, you thrive at the top and keep in control of what is going on around you.

SOCIAL LIFE

Life is wonderful. You meet influential people who are willing to give you a hand and support you.

BUSINESS

You are sharp, and prefer to think before you leap, assessing the possibilities that are available to you. You will always have luck with you.

LOVE

You are romantic and very attractive to the opposite sex. You are always willing to make some extra effort for the ones you love. You know the art of flirtation and know how to make people notice you. As your charm is both deadly and irresistible, you will have the upper hand.

PARENTS

You have considerate and loving parents, but they might demand too much of you, because they believe in you becoming powerful and rich.

SISTERS AND BROTHERS

You will have a good relationship with your siblings, as you know exactly what they want. They look up to you and want you to succeed.

CHILDREN

You are fond of children and can conceive many, but you are also aware of what comes with a child. You will be a good mother or father to your children, as you are very conscientious and loving to them.

TRAVEL
You like travelling, and are especially fond of entertainment. You really enjoy exploring new places. You prefer to have your partner around you when you are on the go, as you love to share happy times with your chosen one.

HEALTH
You are strong and never get sick. The Dragon is so robust that you can look forward to a long life with great happiness with people that you love and care.

INVESTMENTS
Your investments never fail. If you are not too greedy and selfish, you will always make very good money.

TALENTS
You are responsible and efficient. When you are in charge, things seldom fail. Whatever your circumstances you will manage your life and the people in it effectively.

PROSPECTS
You will have a very happy life if you can stop being at times too selfish. Your life is never dull, and you take every day as a new challenge. You love life and enjoy every second of it.

What Kind of Dragon Are You?

THE WOOD DRAGON 1904, 1964
This is the Dragon who likes to participate in parties. You know how to really run the show. You are good at getting things done, for both yourself and your closest ones. You will have a life full of excitement and be spared from dangers and difficulties. Your partner, whom you meet late in life, will appreciate you dearly.

THE FIRE DRAGON 1916, 1976
This is the Dragon in the sky, who will be both powerful and famous. There is a great chance for you to find an outstanding partner, and when the time comes you can be very rich and fortunate. You manage well on your own, and do not need any help from outsiders.

THE EARTH DRAGON 1928, 1988
This the accommodating Dragon who makes no unnecessary demands. You are enterprising and possess great knowledge in many fields. At work, you know exactly what to do to get things properly done. At the beginning you might have a turbulent period, but when you get older your life will be smooth and comfortable.

THE METAL DRAGON 1940, 2000
This is the Dragon with a bad temper. Luckily you are both wise and brave and you can develop yourself to be quite a leader. Your life goes up and down at the beginning, but you will gain a foothold after all. Your old age will be prosperous and comfortable.

THE WATER DRAGON 1952, 2012
This is the Dragon who finds itself high up in the rainy clouds, where there are many activities and great noise, though you know how to take advantage of any situation you find yourself in. You will have an exciting life. Your old age is calm and comfortable.

The Ascendants of the Dragon

11PM–1AM: THE HOUR OF THE RAT 'ZI'
This is an extremely positive alliance for the Dragon, combining the Rat's intuition and intelligence with the strength of the Dragon; you are never a loser. The Dragon in you loves to be adored, adulated and admired, so the Rat's passion will act like a balm on your scales, like cool rain on hot, dry breath.

1AM–3AM: THE HOUR OF THE OX 'ZHOU'
The Dragon is synonymous with good luck. You are extremely intelligent but are inclined to impose your own patterns of life on others. With the Ox in you, you will be forced to be more earthbound and carry out your tasks step by step. You are a great leader, and everyone should take you seriously.

3AM–5AM: THE HOUR OF THE TIGER 'YIN'
With this kind of combination you will be audacious, equipped with a lively and shrewd intelligence. You can be rather bad tempered and hysterical if things do not work out according to

your plans. The impulsive ways of the Tiger are very apparent in your character, but if you take things one step at a time you will go far. This is a very enterprising Dragon indeed.

5am–7am: the Hour of the Rabbit 'Mao'
This is a quiet and peaceful Dragon, with great depth and sound reason. You combine strength with diplomacy and intelligence, which makes you a formidable opponent in any battle.

7am–9am: the Hour of the Dragon 'Zhen'
You are full of energy and never rest. Your path of life is strewn with scales, volcanic earth and tumultuous torrents. Learn to relax, or you may crack up. Join a class in Tai Chi or Qikung.

9am–11am: the Hour of the Snake 'Si'
You are a lucky and cunning animal, a traveller on whom fortune will smile. What you cannot obtain through charm or force, you will acquire through malice or enchantment. In other words you are a formidable beast, full of charm. You will bring a taste of mystery to your partner, who will shiver with either pleasure or fear.

11am–1pm: the Hour of the Horse 'Wu'
This is an exciting combination, where you combine elegance with opportunism, luck with lively intelligence. Few can overcome you. Riding may have its charm, but mounting a Dragon presents inherent dangers that are best avoided by others. You are destined to ride on your own and achieve great success in life.

1pm–3pm: the Hour of the Goat 'Wei'
The Goat in you brings reality and substance to the Dragon's wildest dreams, offering fantasy, imagination and a sense of the marvellous on a platter of clouds. Often too serious, the Dragon will learn to relax and enjoy himself. You are a Dragon who loves comfortable living without worries.

3pm–5pm: the Hour of the Monkey 'Shen'
Possessing a combination of the supremely gifted synchronized with a talent and taste for walking the tightrope, the Dragon/Monkey combination – a valiant and fearless guardian – will never unbuckle his armour. You are always prepared for war; your days and nights are spent in a state of alertness. You

have charm and brilliance and your intelligence is remarkable. Your main defect is your immoderate pride.

5 PM–7 PM: THE HOUR OF THE ROOSTER 'YU'

This is a proud and imaginative Dragon. You possess the bravery of the Rooster. Nothing is better for you than being able to dominate, control and supervise in all circumstances. One thing is for sure – nobody will get bored when you are around.

7 PM–9 PM: THE HOUR OF THE DOG 'XU'

You are the one who inspires confidence, and with reason. One can give you friendship and rely on your words. With this combination you are a loyal, dedicated and faithful animal who appreciates the luck available for you throughout life.

9 PM–11 PM: THE HOUR OF THE PIG 'HAI'

With the Pig alongside the Dragon, you are a solitary wanderer, seeking a treasure that perhaps you did not know how to protect. You will tend to gain material and spiritual wealth. Your life will never be dull.

The Year Ahead

You are very fortunate if you are born in this sign. Most Chinese would prefer to have been born in the Year of the Dragon, because the Dragon means luck and fortune, good health and status. The Dragon has always been the symbol of the Chinese Emperors, the Sons of Heaven, so you are very lucky to have the Dragon as your birth sign.

You are very proud and lively, radiating a strong sense of self-confidence. It is quite obvious that you are intelligent and quick to use all possibilities to your advantage. You are ambitious and firm in everything you do, and you are quite a perfectionist. In one way or another, you tend to be somewhat too prickly and arrogant, and prefer to adopt high standards for yourself. You will always reach the top if you have made up your mind in any career you prefer to make.

You are very serious in everything you do. You dislike silly things and don't mind being critical in order to get things done in the right way. You choose to be very direct in your views and sometimes you can be less diplomatic than you should. Further-more, you could also be very naïve. However, if someone has abused your confidence, you will have difficulty in forgetting, and you like to hit back at a later stage.

You are elegant and have a very attractive attitude, and not least because of your outgoing and positive manner. You will have no difficulties attracting attention and publicity. You enjoy being in the limelight and love to handle difficult questions and problems or find yourself under pressure.

Your energy seems to be endless. You can work hard to get what you want. However you tend to live for the moment, so that you are not capable of seeing the consequences of your actions. You hate to wait and you hate to see things lying around.

You have great confidence and strongly believe in yourself. Though this might lead you to make mistakes at times, you are quick to make repairs and suitable adaptations. You will always be blessed with luck and fortune, so you seldom suffer from anything. Your personality can occasionally be very aggressive. With such willpower and a strong desire to get to the top, you are compelled to succeed.

You have an intense belief in your own judgement and easily overlook others' good advice. You prefer to be independent and let other people see what you are really good at. No wonder it takes some time for you to choose the right partner before you finally settle down. There will be no lack of admirers, and many people will be attracted to your elegance and charisma. As a Dragon you will find people born in the year of the Snake, the Rat, the Monkey and the Rooster very interesting and compatible. You will have a fair chance with the Horse, the Goat, the Ox or the Pig, but try at all costs to avoid the Dog or the Tiger. If not, you will soon discover that you will have so many differences that maintaining a relationship is rather difficult and trying.

The female Dragon is responsible and intelligent and possesses an iron will and energy that many will envy. No job is too small for you; you are good at keeping things on the track at home and out in your career. You are a hard worker and know how to make use of your time. You like to work at home and also out among other people.

You have many exciting interests. You like being outdoors and love sports. You are especially attracted to nature and water. The best pilots are born under this sign, as the Dragon loves to fly. Travel to unknown places is your passion, and you are very adventurous. Success will literally fall into your lap; all you have to do is to make use of all possibilities. Besides, your positive attitude will win you many friends and you will always find yourself at the centre of attention. Your charm is often a source of inspiration for other people around you. In other words, you are a very successful person with many adventures ahead.

You will have a very comfortable year, but you will have to take great care of your health. You will experience a more relaxed relationship with life. You will have a great supply of physical energies, making you warm and receptive. In most cases, you like to share your ideas and possibilities with your close ones. A quiet and pleasant period, with no problems, financial setbacks or bad news, is awaiting you this year.

Week By Week For People Born Under the Sign of the Dragon

5–11 FEBRUARY 2000 (5 FEBRUARY:
CHINESE NEW YEAR – YEAR OF THE DRAGON)

Domestic arguments over insignificant issues are likely. Married Dragons particularly have to watch their temper. Do not be overly critical of your partner and avoid interfering with the way family members are handling their work. Do not adopt a bossy or dictatorial attitude.

Your lucky numbers this week: 1, 12, 13, 31.

12–18 FEBRUARY 2000

This should be a happy and successful week for socializing. Pay more attention to pleasure than to regular work. It is likely that you have been ignoring the wishes of your family, to a certain extent; do all that you can to remedy the situation now. There will be opportunities to work on creative projects that will mean a great deal to you but will not interfere with romantic moments with your chosen one.

Your lucky numbers this week: 14, 15, 26, 30.

19–25 FEBRUARY 2000

Nothing of great significance is likely during this rather quiet week. This is not a good week for making a long journey and avoid activities with large groups of people. Do what you can to make this period a pleasant week for your immediate family.

Your lucky numbers this week: 1, 16, 23, 35.

26 FEBRUARY–3 MARCH 2000

You need to tread warily. There are a number of pitfalls to look out for. The cash situation requires careful handling and numerous regular bills are coming up for payment now. You may find your reserves falling rather drastically, but a letter received this week should bring good news.

Your lucky numbers this week: 1, 12, 15, 26.

4–10 MARCH 2000

Nervous tension will ease. You should feel more rested. Problems that were most vexing last week may not be quite so difficult to overcome. You will find friends and relatives most helpful and advice from people older than yourself should be reassuring. No important financial moves ought to be made this week.

Your lucky numbers this week: 14, 16, 26, 32.

11–17 MARCH 2000

Mental agility can be combined with physical exertion to produce exceptional results. Do what you can to increase your knowledge in areas that could earn you more money later. Younger Dragons who are unhappy in their work should look around for other ways to earn a living.

Your lucky numbers this week: 6, 9, 15, 30.

18–24 MARCH 2000

Influential people will sit up and take notice of what you say. You have a greater chance than usual to win support from above. Agreements made now will allow steady progress with a creative enterprise. More routine work is unlikely to progress quite so smoothly this week though.

Your lucky numbers this week: 10, 11, 26, 34.

25–31 MARCH 2000

This will be a slow week. Your biggest danger could be boredom. If you find yourself at a loose end, try to involve yourself in something productive as too much spare time could lead to the seeking of extravagant pleasure. There may be differences of opinion at home. If you are dating someone for the first time, be careful not to be too aggressive.

Your lucky numbers this week: 14, 15, 26, 31.

1 APRIL–7 APRIL 2000

One of the best weeks of the month for things on the home front. An about turn by loved ones means that you can make steady progress with jobs you are keen to tackle in the house. Health problems can be sorted out. You should be feeling in much better shape physically.

Your lucky numbers this week: 1, 4, 26, 36.

8–14 APRIL 2000

This week can be used for catching up with neglected tasks. Though you had a fairly busy time last week, you will still have to sort out things that have been left behind. Romance will be no problem this week either. Your love life may not be very exciting at the moment, but you will be grateful for the security of your present relationship.

Your lucky numbers this week: 14, 18, 26, 27.

15–21 APRIL 2000

Unexpected income could come your way. Do what you can to make money from creative enterprises. Hobbies may easily become part-time jobs. See what you can do to win support for your new ideas from people in a position to help you. Romance will be exciting and stimulating this week.

Your lucky numbers this week: 11, 19, 26, 31.

22–28 APRIL 2000

A useful week for contacting people who are not always easy to see. Influential colleagues may be able to hook you up with someone who can be of special benefit to your career. It would be best not to make an inflexible timetable this week.

Your lucky numbers this week: 10, 13, 26, 32.

29 APRIL–5 MAY 2000

No pressure will be placed on you this week. You will respond well to the added responsibility of choosing your own pace at work. Superiors will be too busy to listen to new ideas that you are keen to promote. Stick to routine matters for the time being.

Your lucky numbers this week: 1, 14, 26, 33.

6–12 MAY 2000

Work activities are extremely sensitive. Colleagues do not see eye-to-eye with you, and, try as you might, it will be virtually impossible to have your ideas accepted by them. No changes in work patterns should be attempted. Do not make any impulsive decisions about love affairs.

Your lucky numbers this week: 10, 26, 31, 32.

13–19 MAY 2000

This week will be marked by a lack of activity. Friction is unlikely, which will certainly come as a welcome relief. Your partner will agree with most of your ideas for the week. It looks as if you may be spending more time at home than usual. Give your attention to older relatives.

Your lucky numbers this week: 14, 15, 20, 22.

20–26 MAY 2000

Early confusion could slow you down. Do not place too much faith in promises made by associates. Colleagues are likely to be unpredictable, and promises made verbally may be conveniently forgotten. Forge ahead with creative enterprises.

Your lucky numbers this week: 11, 15, 26, 31.

27 MAY–2 JUNE 2000

A lack of energy could make this a rather slow week. You will have some difficulty getting into top gear. Money matters need to be approached with caution, and you cannot afford extravagant impulses. Problems of loved ones could create unavoidable expenses this week.

Your lucky numbers this week: 17, 19, 29, 32.

3–9 JUNE 2000

Another difficult week ahead. In the areas of romance and finance you have to be extremely cautious. Be on guard at all times and take no situation for granted. One false move now could upset carefully laid plans for the future.

Your lucky numbers this week: 6, 14, 15, 26.

10–16 JUNE 2000

A expensive week. You will be shelling out more money than intended on entertainment, thanks to the insistence of friends.

Try not to spend in an attempt to impress. Take care if travelling; there could be minor accidents or brushes with the law. Drivers should check their vehicles before setting off.

Your lucky numbers this week: 4, 19, 20, 36.

17–23 JUNE 2000

A good week for getting back to the daily grind. Routine matters will not overly tax your mind and important decisions can be taken without worries. Work colleagues may not be too friendly; check out their likely reactions before asking for favours.

Your lucky numbers this week: 14, 15, 26, 31.

24–30 JUNE 2000

Those involved in any kind of legal proceedings will find satisfactory results coming their way this week. However, be careful to remain on the right side of the law, since you may become involved again. This weekend favours all those connected with arts or the entertainment business.

Your lucky numbers this week: 1, 2, 14, 25.

1 JULY–7 JULY 2000

A week of good news. Expect financial rewards for previous good work. Your mail will also prove to be important; throw nothing away until you have read it thoroughly. The weekend is a good time for romance. Younger Dragons will find parents restrictive and unco-operative.

Your lucky numbers this week: 1, 6, 7, 8, 29.

8–14 JULY 2000

Pay attention to matters of domestic importance that you have been ignoring all week. Now it is time to get things settled on the home front. If partners have been unco-operative, you should find them less so this week. Romance is likely this weekend.

Your lucky numbers this week: 1, 14, 15, 26.

15–21 JULY 2000

You do not have to fight very hard for what you want this week, so it is an excellent time for asking for favours from superiors. Try to refrain from asking for financial help; this can come later. This weekend a member of the opposite sex will be of particular help.

Your lucky numbers this week: 2, 3, 26, 36.

22–28 July 2000

Whatever is happening at work will affect you later this week. Try to keep abreast of what is going on. Colleagues are evasive and unco-operative, so you will have to do your own investigations. Domestic problems interfere with entertainment this weekend.

Your lucky numbers this week: 10, 15, 29, 33.

29 July–4 August 2000

Imagination and intuition can be used with effect this week. Any brainwaves you have at present should be written down for future reference. Those involved in creative jobs should have an excellent week, full of original thoughts. Hunches should be acted upon and new ideas tested.

Your lucky numbers this week: 1, 19, 26, 34.

5–11 August 2000

This is a good week for completing outstanding business. Clear away routine work and deal with more important items as soon as possible. Do not let stick-in-the-mud colleagues stand in your way. Your judgement is reliable at present, so follow your instincts.

Your lucky numbers this week: 2, 4, 15, 30.

12–18 August 2000

Conditions at your workplace should be going in your favour and you have the power to change things so that you benefit. Financially this not a good week for taking gambles or getting involved in anything of a speculative nature. Keep your cash in your pocket wherever possible.

Your lucky numbers this week: 3, 11, 26, 36.

19–25 August 2000

Romance undergoes a specially rocky time this week. Permanent partnerships will also encounter problems. If you are suddenly attracted to a member of the opposite sex, make certain that you are able to deliver what you should. This is not a time to put relationships in jeopardy.

Your lucky numbers this week: 6, 17, 19, 30.

26 August–1 September 2000

A work week that drags by slowly. Routine concerns seem to be unnecessarily and you are thwarted by interfering colleagues.

Try not to lose your temper as you will come out the worse for wear if you become involved in an argument. Confrontations with marriage partners should also be avoided.

Your lucky numbers this week: 10, 15, 26, 33.

2–8 SEPTEMBER 2000
A week of tension, not helped by pressures of work. Your load will be heavier than normal and you will find yourself struggling towards the end of the week. This weekend should be spent in the company of people who relax and humour you.

Your lucky numbers this week: 4, 18, 29, 35.

9–15 SEPTEMBER 2000
You will find it difficult to get into full swing at your place of employment. Colleagues will not be inclined to fall in with your ideas and you will have to seek new ways to accomplish things. The week will demand your flexibility and diplomatic way of doing things.

Your lucky numbers this week: 14, 15, 26, 31.

16–22 SEPTEMBER 2000
Avoid wasting time and energy this week, as you will need all your strength for a potentially exhausting business trip. Go off the beaten track to get things done. Your boss will appreciate your aggressive attitude in pulling in new business.

Your lucky numbers this week: 1, 10, 26, 27.

23–29 SEPTEMBER 2000
Matters concerning people and places abroad will be highest in your mind this week. Good news from overseas can be expected and if you are involved in the travel industry you can expect to have a successful and profitable week. Those about to embark on a protracted trip have chosen a good time to do so.

Your lucky numbers this week: 2, 3, 4, 18.

30 SEPTEMBER–6 OCTOBER 2000
Travel is still prominent, although this week it favours those making short trips. Commercial travellers and representatives will have a profitable week without journeying too far afield. The housewife or househusband will find bargains close to home. Romance can also be found while travelling.

Your lucky numbers this week: 1, 3, 15, 16.

7–13 October 2000

Do not take promises too seriously this week, especially if they are made by someone with whom you are romantically involved. Superiors are also prone to making promises they cannot keep. Trust only yourself. Lending money this week will lead to problems.

Your lucky numbers this week: 2, 4, 15, 26.

14–20 October 2000

Pay attention to events in your personal life as these will have a bearing on your career. Partners may seem happy, but they are hiding something from you. This week you should attempt to sort out any family differences that have arisen lately.

Your lucky numbers this week: 1, 11, 26, 33.

21–27 October 2000

Meet people halfway and aim for compromise solutions wherever you can. You will not progress far if you try to go it alone. This is the right time to think about the future. Pay attention to matters of security in old age. Invest in your own future rather than splurging on items of short-lived value.

Your lucky numbers this week: 3, 14, 15, 20.

28 October–3 November 2000

An excellent period for all romantic matters. You are clearly able to let your partner know how you feel about any aspect of life, and you have more than enough cheek to carry out a daring personal plan. When you need support, you should find that it is ready and waiting in the wings. This is a period for action.

Your lucky numbers this week: 1, 14, 26, 36.

4–10 November 2000

This is another busy week. Make certain that you know what is expected of you in advance. Nobody can really tell you how to behave at the moment, even if that is exactly what most people seem to be doing. By the weekend a new attitude to an old problem can help you out no end.

Your lucky numbers this week: 4, 6, 18, 30.

11–17 November 2000

Do not be reluctant about thinking big, because there is every chance that you can make your most grandiose schemes pay off this week. Reactions are highly supportive, which leads you to believe that you can get away with almost anything that occurs to you.

Your lucky numbers this week: 14, 15, 26, 31.

18–24 NOVEMBER 2000

Things are still looking good, though the coming weekend probably puts a brake on practical activities. Turn your attention and your plans towards your personal life, which looks more exciting than it has done for ages. Remove obstacles from your personal path quickly.

Your lucky numbers this week: 5, 6, 26, 31.

25 NOVEMBER–1 DECEMBER 2000

You should now have more time to spend upon the more practical aspects of life. You can even turn rather difficult situations to your advantage. It is only a matter of time before you discover that a difficult problem is about to be solved, and you will be pleased to do some serious thinking on behalf of a friend.

Your lucky numbers this week: 3, 5, 8, 30.

2–8 DECEMBER 2000

Your energy is at a high level this week and you will not be interested in domestic chores and other small jobs around the house. This is a good time to plan a change of décor. If you are invited out this weekend by a member of the opposite sex, be on your best behaviour and make a good impression.

Your lucky numbers this week: 14, 15, 26, 33.

9–15 DECEMBER 2000

The emphasis this week seems to be placed on pleasure. There probably will not be quite the level of time for practical considerations that this period might demand of you. Keep track of finances, which are probably not very strong at the moment. It will not be long before they improve at the end of the week.

Your lucky numbers this week: 21, 31, 32, 36.

16–22 DECEMBER 2000

Career issues can seem to be more trouble than they are worth at present. Take one situation at a time and, when possible, leave major decisions alone. Remember that you are only human and that you need to listen as well as talk. Short-term plans should be turning out as you wish.

Your lucky numbers this week: 4, 15, 26, 34.

23–29 DECEMBER 2000

This week social contacts with a wider range of people become likely. For some Dragons there will be new romantic involvements in store, possibly with people from other cultures or backgrounds. A generally optimistic approach to life works best, and can bring positive trends before long.

Your lucky numbers this week: 11, 22, 23, 28.

30 DECEMBER 2000–5 JANUARY 2001

Good news could arrive regarding personal plans for travel or journeys of any sort. All in all, this should prove to be a useful sort of week, even if it is not possible to achieve as much practically as you would wish. Domestic routines should be avoided if they seem too much of a chore.

Your lucky numbers this week: 1, 7, 9, 10.

6–12 JANUARY 2001

Your powers of attraction should be fairly high at the moment. If you are looking for love, it will not be hard to find and the general impression that you make on the world means that you carry great influence. Ask what you want of others, because they are unlikely to say no.

Your lucky numbers this week: 14, 17, 26, 35.

13–19 JANUARY 2001

Great optimism comes your way, together with an enthusiasm associated with friendship. Past disappointments are now quite properly forgotten and pleasant surprises result from happenings within the family. Concern over the well-being of younger people could be quite misplaced.

Your lucky numbers this week: 2, 15, 26, 35.

20–26 JANUARY 2001 (24 JANUARY: CHINESE NEW YEAR – YEAR OF THE SNAKE)

Most of your attention needs to be turned towards career prospects and practicalities. When faced with a number of uncertainties, you may be inclined to opt for what you really understand. It would be worthwhile trying to get to know why loved ones feel the way they do this week.

Your lucky numbers this week: 14, 19, 26, 31.

THE SIGN OF THE
Snake

The Chinese name for the Snake: Si
The sixth sign in the Chinese zodiac
The hours governed by the Snake: 9am–11am
The corresponding sign in the Western zodiac: Virgo
Element: Fire
The direction of the pole: Negative

*

The Year of the Snake in the Western Calendar

4 February 1905–24 January 1906 Wood Snake
23 January 1917–10 February 1918 Fire Snake
10 February 1929–29 January 1930 Earth Snake
27 January 1941–14 February 1942 Metal Snake
14 February 1953–2 February 1954 Water Snake
2 February 1965–20 January 1966 Wood Snake
18 February 1977–6 February 1978 Fire Snake
6 February 1989–26 January 1990 Earth Snake
24 January 2001–11 February 2001 Metal Snake

Famous People Born Under the Sign of the Snake

Muhammad Ali, Ann-Margret, Yassir Arafat, Kim Basinger, Tony Blair, Benazir Bhutto, Randy Crawford, Charles Darwin, Bob Dylan, Stefan Edberg, Sir Alexander Fleming, Henry Fonda, Greta Garbo, Art Garfunkel, J. Paul Getty, Goethe, Princess Grace of Monaco, Audrey Hepburn, Jack Higgins, Paul Hogan, Howard Hughes, Liz Hurley, J.F. Kennedy, Carole King, Mao Zedong, Dean Martin, Henri Matisse, Robert Mitchum, Gamal Nasser, Alfred Nobel, Mike Oldfield, Aristotle Onassis, Jacqueline Onassis, Ryan O'Neal, Dorothy Parker, Pablo Picasso, Mary Pickford, Brad Pitt, Gerhard Schröder, Franz Schubert, Brooke Shields, Paul Simon, Dionne Warwick, Oprah Winfrey, Virginia Woolf, Susannah York.

The Snake in a Nutshell

POSITIVE QUALITIES
Considerate, wise, deep, patient, quick-witted, psychic, organized and very good at planning.

NEGATIVE QUALITIES
Demanding, like to rule, can be very jealous and sometimes lazy. At times you tend to be very closed and reserved.

CAREER SUGGESTIONS
You would make a good artist, politician or consultant or work in any profession dealing with superstition and fortune-telling.

Main Features of the Snake

You are detailed and have a good sense of control, but you tend to be very conceited and egotistic. Remember it is wise to think of others as well, and not just of yourself. Just like the Snake, you are sensitive and smart.

LUCK
You prefer to make things happen on your own and make serious efforts to get on in life. It is very seldom that you will have any problems, and you are always focused about matters concerning the opposite sex.

MONEY

You work best with your own methods and are good at taking care of your own resources. You can be very rich in the later stages of life.

WORK

You are a very good administrator, clever at putting your ideas into action. You are also a very good adviser and a counsellor, because you can always see things from different angles.

SOCIAL LIFE

You are fond of nightlife on the one hand, but enjoy solitude on the other. In other words, it is up to you to decide what you like to do on any particular day.

BUSINESS

You are observant and capable. You always see possibilities and manage to hang on to them. Your life is a constant challenge and you manage to stay on top in every difficult situation.

LOVE

You are demanding and you usually devote time to finding the right partner. Too often you set yourself ambitious goals, and it is wise to downgrade your expectations.

PARENTS

Usually you will have very loving parents, but you like to do things in your own way. Some Snakes will have very strict parents, so childhood might be very trying.

SISTERS AND BROTHERS

You often have a good relationship with siblings if you try not to be too dominant, though you are kind and willing to sacrifice some of your resources to make the relationship succeed.

CHILDREN

You love your children dearly and do everything you can for them, though this might create hurt for yourself. You strive for a good and harmonious family life with your closest ones.

TRAVEL

Travel is a must; it is both a joy and passion. You like to meet new people and go to places you never have been to before. In other words, you are adventurous.

HEALTH
You have good health, but can be prone to stress and allergies if you do not take care. Furthermore, you will need to chew your food properly before swallowing, in order to avoid digestive problems.

INVESTMENTS
You are a speculator and know exactly when and how to invest in order to earn a healthy profit.

TALENTS
You are generally considerate and wise, but sometimes you can be very demanding and then nothing seems good enough for you. However, you would make a good teacher or instructor whatever your chosen profession.

PROSPECTS
If you stop being so demanding and speculative, then friends will flock around you and you will lead a very good and prosperous life.

What Kind of Snake Are You?

THE WOOD SNAKE 1905, 1965
This Snake is creeping out from its hiding place. You are a very honest and straightforward person, both sociable and pleasant to talk to. You love power and are a very capable administrator.

THE FIRE SNAKE 1917, 1977
This is the Snake in open terrain. You possess a strong sense of righteousness and prefer to deal in the open. You are both elegant and intelligent. When you get older, you life will be harmonious and without worries.

THE EARTH SNAKE 1929, 1989
This is a happy Snake, full of reason and wisdom, but at the same time active, with the prospects to go far. You are lucky in your choice of partner, and fortune will smile on you.

THE METAL SNAKE 1941, 2001
This is the sleeping Snake. You are clever but too sensitive, at the same time you are ambitious enough to handle any kind of

opportunities in your favour. You seldom make any mistakes, but should you fail, you will not give up.

THE WATER SNAKE 1953, 2013

This is the Snake from the woods. You are intelligent and generous, but somewhat naïve too. There will be many exciting experiences and problems in your youth, but after that you will enjoy a strong and constructive period.

The Ascendants of the Snake

11PM–1AM: THE HOUR OF THE RAT 'ZI'

You are usually a charming, sweet little Snake with its tongue kept in place. However, you can be rather poisonous when provoked. You are very sentimental and especially clever when it comes to dealing with money.

1AM–3AM: THE HOUR OF THE OX 'ZHOU'

This is a very good combination: you are stable and diligent, but have an irresistible charm. You are pretty clever and, possessing the strength of the Ox, you will go far. This makes for an invincible pair, especially if the Ox tries to get things done without too much hesitation.

3AM–5AM: THE HOUR OF THE TIGER 'YIN'

You are the professional charmer, crafty and sly if the need arises, capable of biting and releasing venom in order to attain your ends. At the same time the Snake in you fights the Tiger fiercely, and you are occasionally at a loss about what to do. Either you are very confident and optimistic, or you are depressed and uncertain.

5AM–7AM: THE HOUR OF THE RABBIT 'MAO'

Although you may be a soft and flattering Snake, you are not easy to understand – especially when you tend to become rather poisonous and moody. The Rabbit in you can make it difficult to get along with yourself. Nobody knows if you will be pleased or upset, but one thing is clear: nobody wants to be bitten by you.

7AM–9AM: THE HOUR OF THE DRAGON 'ZHEN'

You are a lucky and cunning animal. This combination makes a traveller on whom fortune will smile. What you cannot obtain by force or charm you will obtain by malice and enchantment. You are both a commander-in-chief and someone who understands the application of strategy and tactics.

9AM–11AM: THE HOUR OF THE SNAKE 'SI'

With the Snake as your ascendant, you tend to be both very possessive and very mysterious. Not many people understand you, but one thing is for sure – whatever you choose to do, you will go for it with great courage. Although, as a Snake, you may be slow, you will succeed in the end.

11AM–1PM: THE HOUR OF THE HORSE 'WU'

This is a wise and good-natured Snake who always sees the bright side of life. As both the Horse and the Snake enjoy sex, it is no wonder that you will have many exciting adventures.

1PM–3PM: THE HOUR OF THE GOAT 'WEI'

It certainly will be fatal to fall in love with you. It is impossible to expect fidelity from this Snake/Goat combination. In life you will enjoy plenty of good luck and have the advantage of good taste as well as a capacity for finesse, but your instability will be a burden for you through life.

3PM–5PM: THE HOUR OF THE MONKEY 'SHEN'

You are either a genius who knows how to make use of your talents, or you are a little devil who wants to mob others. In any case, you are quite simply irresistible and difficult to handle. This combination makes for a good talker and hero, or, at the other extreme, a liar and swindler.

5PM–7PM: THE HOUR OF THE ROOSTER 'YU'

You are a group leader and a person who, under your colourful feathers, harbours a taste for unlimited power. You are diligent and possess a deep knowledge in many fields. You are also intuitive and frank. Through life, you will be able to accomplish much with your generous heart, good will and honesty. Your life will never be dull.

7PM–9PM: THE HOUR OF THE DOG 'XU'

With this combination you are courageous and warm and understand the meaning of faithfulness. You have a keen moral sense and are intuitive, but you have a tendency to be rather pessimistic. Life with you can become very complicated. You are the kind to torment yourself to excess, announcing the onset of a hurricane when the wind picks up, or expecting a deluge after a few drops of rain.

9PM–11PM: THE HOUR OF THE PIG 'HAI'

Though you are peace-loving, secretive and sensitive, you are also a poor loser and prefer solitude to risking failure. You also tend to have difficulties in making decisions; sometimes the Pig in you will trick the Snake, so that you land yourself in trouble.

The Year Ahead

You are endowed with wisdom and beauty in equally large proportions. Your mind is forever active, as you seek the answers to many universal questions. You are always well organized, alert and reflective. People born under this sign are elegant and beautiful and understand the art of seduction. The childhood of the Snake will be happy, though only if calmness reigns within the family, otherwise this age will be critical. Youth will be free of problems, though in maturity you will be at the mercy of all kinds of passions and your emotional life will often be unstable. In old age you will finally profit from his wisdom, although the fires of love will die slowly and are likely to cause you problems for a long time.

Snakes are intuitive; one can even speak of a 'sixth sense'. As the Snake you instinctively feel things before they occur and detect the inner thoughts of others when in conversation. All this, along with your imagination and mental alertness, makes you well armed for the battle of life.

Your behaviour is calm and peaceful, for you love harmony and stability. You are also adaptable, well balanced and blessed with a firm will, which you reveal without hesitation when your moral or material comfort is threatened, reacting with the same vindictive vivacity as if someone were stepping on your tail. When you do have nothing to do, you can be amazingly lazy. You will tend to take it easy and enjoy sleeping, waking late in the morning.

As the Snake you are lucky. Happily you often win your battles, for you are a bad loser. You take failure as a personal affront and do not tolerate insults. At the same time, you are an understanding and far-sighted adviser, who likes to help your friends – as long as money is not involved, for you can be very stingy. But you adore being asked for help. The Snake has certain defects; you do not like to listen to a word of what is being said to you. Nor do you take advice. You like to run your own show.

The female Snake is exclusive and jealous, and loves to feel she is the centre of the universe in her partner's eyes. Fidelity is another question. You have a very individual conception of it, but in most circumstances you prefer to retain a minimum of liberty and independence.

Both the male and the female Snakes possess a profound need to please and attract, which gives you the impression that you truly exist. It is natural for you to behave charmingly, but this must not be exploited; if you are victim of a jealous scene, you will become even more distant and move even further away. Snakes are sensual and passionate and blossom in relationships based as much on physical compatibility as on dialogue.

As the Snake you love money because it furnishes you the lifestyle you want – surrounding yourself with pretty objects, holidaying around the world, buying expensive clothes and all the books and music you might wish. And whatever you want and desire, you will get! Being a lucky and resolute social climber, you can be relied on to achieve a certain affluence; you rarely lack money. You are the most opportunistic of all the signs and know how to seize the valuable opportunity and leave aside lesser attractions.

This is not a year of optimism and pleasure. You become more serious and introverted, and at times tend to shut people out. In love you could be cold and unnatural, because you demand too much of your surroundings. You are vulnerable and sensitive; maybe you react in the wrong way. Even minor conflicts with your partner have a tendency to drag along without end. You want to do things in your own way and are difficult to understand. It is wise of you to divide your tasks into sections so that things can be accomplished one step at a time. At the beginning of the year you will have problems in getting things done, and you will spend more money than you can really afford. If you try to change this attitude, things will work out all right for you after all.

Week By Week For People Born Under the Sign of the Snake

5–11 FEBRUARY 2000 (5 FEBRUARY: CHINESE NEW YEAR – YEAR OF THE DRAGON)

Make a special effort to clear out the dead wood in your life this week. Unwanted friendships and acquaintances should be terminated in order to make room for new people. You will benefit from the advice of a stranger this weekend; keep your ears open during all casual conversations.

Your lucky numbers this week: 14, 21, 29, 32.

12–18 FEBRUARY 2000

Helpful and heart-warming news is on the way, probably from a good friend abroad. The positive side is that you can use what is being said as a platform for your own plans. Creating more space for yourself is also a part of the scenario of what should be a positive week.

Your lucky numbers this week: 1, 19, 29, 34.

19–25 FEBRUARY 2000

What happens at work this week will upset your calculations for months ahead. You may have to lower your sights temporarily. Do not be disillusioned, however; things will work out to your advantage. This weekend is a bad time for romance. Partners are likely to be difficult and argumentative.

Your lucky numbers this week: 1, 10, 21, 23.

26 FEBRUARY–3 MARCH 2000

Things are likely to slow down a little bit for the beginning of the week, but this is only short-term. You tend to have a shortage of both energy and time, so it would be practical to find ways and means of using both most fruitfully.

Your lucky numbers this week: 6, 17, 28, 29, 32.

4–10 MARCH 2000

You can turn invitations to good account now. It matters not if the proposals come in your business life or whether they are social ones, you cannot turn them down. Although it is still some time away, you may well have your sights firmly fixed on the summer period and your hopes for it.

Your lucky numbers this week: 1, 8, 9, 29.

11–17 MARCH 2000

With potentially exciting things happening in all areas of life this week, there is nothing to prevent you from being cheerful and positive in your general approach. Not everyone is inclined to agree with you at present, but you have the persuasive powers to bring almost anyone round to your point of view this week.

Your lucky numbers this week: 15, 26, 28, 30.

18–24 MARCH 2000

Meet people halfway and look for compromise solutions wherever you can. You will not achieve much if you try to do things alone. This is the right time to think about the future, so pay attention to matters concerning security in later life. Invest in your own future, rather than splurging on things of short-lived value.

Your lucky numbers this week: 1, 26, 27, 32.

25–31 MARCH 2000

An excellent period for romance. You are clearly able to let your partner know how you feel concerning just about any aspect of life and have more than enough cheek to carry out a daring personal plan. When you need support, you should find that it is ready and waiting in the wings. This is a period to act.

Your lucky numbers this week: 2, 7, 18, 29.

1 APRIL–7 APRIL 2000

This is another busy week for Snakes, but be sure that you know what is expected of you in advance. Nobody can tell you how to behave at the moment, even if that is exactly what most individuals seem to be doing. A fresh attitude to an old problem can help you out no end by the weekend.

Your lucky numbers this week: 2, 4, 23, 28.

8–14 APRIL 2000

Do not shirk from thinking big, because there is every chance that you can make your most grandiose schemes pay off this week. The reaction of people in your vicinity is extraordinary, leading you to believe that you have the potential to achieve almost anything that occurs to you.

Your lucky numbers this week: 1, 3, 23, 28.

15–21 APRIL 2000

Everything seems to look good, though practical matters are probably slowing down a little as the weekend approaches. You should now turn your attention towards plans for your personal life, which looks more exciting than it has done for ages. Remove any obstacles from your personal path quickly.

Your lucky numbers this week: 2, 10, 23, 29.

22–28 APRIL 2000

You will have to make deep reflections on your own situation on personal matters. This does not prevent you from being yourself and from doing what comes naturally in business and socially. You might feel like a change of scene after work and can spend time with a special person.

Your lucky numbers this week: 1, 5, 16, 27.

29 APRIL–5 MAY 2000

Family matters will now take up most of your time, leaving little room to create the practical space you need to advance your career. Patience is required, but you might find it hard to find within yourself just at the moment. Experience and common sense count in most situations right now.

Your lucky numbers this week: 3, 26, 27, 30.

6–12 MAY 2000

Private matters continue to take up much of your time. You may be planning to spend more time with your closest ones this week. Meanwhile you need to conclude various practical dealings, so that you can pick up the baton next week in a more positive way.

Your lucky numbers this week: 1, 6, 7, 30.

13–19 MAY 2000

You should now have more time to devote to the more practical aspects of life. You can even turn rather difficult situations to your own advantage. It is only a matter of time before you realize that a tricky problem is about to find a solution and you will be pleased to put your mind to work for the benefit of a friend.

Your lucky numbers this week: 11, 25, 26, 30.

20–26 May 2000

Fun and pleasure are very important to you this week, so there will probably be little time for practical considerations that might be demanded of you. Keep an eye on finances, which are probably not very strong at the moment. It will not be long before they improve at the end of the week,

Your lucky numbers this week: 12, 23, 34, 36.

27 May–2 June 2000

You may receive some very good news from a friend abroad. This could mark the beginning of new projects in the very near future. You will have a smooth week in which most of your plans and dreams start to materialize.

Your lucky numbers this week: 1, 7, 19, 30.

3–9 June 2000

Unfortunately everything seems to slow down a little bit for you this week. Luckily this seems to be a temporary phase, but in the meantime you are tired and moody. It would be wise to take one step at a time.

Your lucky numbers this week: 2, 3, 4, 18.

10–16 June 2000

A good week for employers to investigate new ways of dealing with staff. If you are involved in the import/export business you can expect the start of a very profitable period. This is a good time to introduce new ranges to prospective customers. Romance is shaky; you should tread very carefully.

Your lucky numbers this week: 15, 26, 27, 30.

17–23 June 2000

You appear to be changing your feelings towards someone in a most drastic manner; if this is the case, make a clean break. Hanging on to crumbling relationships will only lead to sorrow and heartbreak. Work matters are routine, with nothing much to bother you in this field.

Your lucky numbers this week: 1, 14, 26, 36.

24–30 June 2000

A good week for reorganizing things at work. Do not be deterred by gripes from your colleagues; you are doing things the right way. Superiors will be easy to approach. Domestic affairs are still not running smoothly, so discussions with partners could help this state of affairs.

Your lucky numbers this week: 2, 3, 26, 37.

1 JULY–7 JULY 2000

Start the week as you mean to carry on. This is not a good day for changes, so fix your targets and keep to them. You could find that you are shouldering the problems of colleagues, so be strong enough to hand them back if they are too much of a burden. Romance is improving.

Your lucky numbers this week: 1, 2, 4, 35.

8–14 JULY 2000

Caution is required when operating mechanical or electrical machinery. There is a risk of accidents. Take care trying out any new gadget you do not understand. Read any instructions carefully before tampering with instruments that are unknown to you. The best part of the week is from Wednesday onwards. You will not want to stray very far away from home – which is something of a change for you.

Your lucky numbers this week: 4, 5, 7, 28.

15–21 JULY 2000

Do not allow colleagues to exploit your good nature, especially where loans are involved. Lending money now will lead to complications later when you try to reclaim the cash. A broken romance can be healed this weekend.

Your lucky numbers this week: 3, 4, 17, 18.

22–28 JULY 2000

Do not try to complete important business deals this week. It will be difficult to contact or communicate effectively with influential people. Colleagues are not in the mood for hard work. People in your workplace will be congenial enough but may lack the necessary driving force to get anything moving. This week is best used for jobs that can be achieved alone, especially those that require an extra bit of concentration. It is wise to do what you can to improve your relationship with your partner.

Your lucky numbers this week: 8, 15, 26, 30.

29 JULY–4 AUGUST 2000

You may be feeling uncertain about a career development. If you are at all unhappy with things as they stand, consult superiors to find out your next move. Finances could get a small boost midweek. Romance develops along familiar lines this week, though this may not be entirely to your liking.

Your lucky numbers this week: 16, 27, 28, 31.

5–11 AUGUST 2000

You have to be vigilant this week. Being quick-witted, you are not usually taken in by other people, but someone you thought was reliable may try to deceive you. A longstanding colleague may wish to borrow money but do not lend cash without knowing exactly when you are going to recover it and how the payment will be made. If you do not cover yourself where it counts, you could end up as the loser. Devote some time to creative work that gives you an opportunity to make good use of your active imagination.

Your lucky numbers this week: 4, 11, 26, 35.

12–18 AUGUST 2000

It is time that you gave your career plans a jolt. Set things in motion this week, and do not allow weaker colleagues to stand in your way. Romantic encounters in your workplace take on a note of seriousness; make certain that your intended is not spoken for.

Your lucky numbers this week: 1, 15, 26, 33.

19–25 AUGUST 2000

Money matters require cautious handling. People born under this sign must be cautious regarding the persons with whom they have financial dealings. Speculation in any form would be most hazardous. You will have a tendency to be careless with money. Keep personal spending within reasonable limits. Guard your wallet or purse.

Your lucky numbers this week: 1, 19, 26, 32.

26 AUGUST–1 SEPTEMBER 2000

Home and property affairs are badly starred this week. You could find yourself making a serious mistake where a new house or a move is concerned. Avoid signing contracts and make no financial commitments. This weekend will find you in a pensive mood. Do not make your partner's life a misery.

Your lucky numbers this week: 14, 15, 27, 33.

2–8 SEPTEMBER 2000

Buckle down to work early this week and get routine matters out of the way before midweek, as there will be much to achieve later in the week. Enlist the help of an older colleague, should you find it necessary. Younger members of staff are out to stop you getting what you want. Do nothing this weekend that could lead to gossip.

Your lucky numbers this week: 10, 15, 26, 31.

9–15 SEPTEMBER 2000

You will need to slow down. You may be too anxious to move about, so think what so much travel is likely to accomplish. Do not make a journey to see influential people unless you have a confirmed appointment. Much time and expense could be wasted on the move. Conduct business by telephone wherever possible. Be a little more tactful in handling family matters and watch your temper. Say nothing in the heat of the moment that you would immediately regret.

Your lucky numbers this week: 10, 19, 26, 32.

16–22 SEPTEMBER 2000

Family problems can be dealt with this week with the help of a senior member of your family. Put all your cards on the table if you wish to find a solution. Financially, this is not a good week for the gambler, so stakes should be kept within reason. Romance develops along the lines you wish for.

Your lucky numbers this week: 14, 15, 20, 35.

23–29 SEPTEMBER 2000

This quiet week gives you the opportunity to plan future moves. There is unlikely to be any great pressure from above now. No new problems will develop in your regular job and everything routine should progress steadily. This is an excellent week to allow your natural talents to develop freely.

Your lucky numbers this week: 1, 21, 26, 33.

30 SEPTEMBER–6 OCTOBER 2000

Much that seemed impossible to achieve within the family circle will be accomplished this week, but only if you are prepared to give and take; a selfish attitude will go against you. Unwanted relationships from your past will surface again this weekend, much to your displeasure.

Your lucky numbers this week: 12, 14, 26, 34.

7–13 OCTOBER 2000

This week is going to be busy, so prepare yourself for some hard work, though it will work in your favour so you should put yourself out wherever possible. Jealous relatives cause problems and arguments between you and loved ones this weekend. Younger members of the family are also difficult.

Your lucky numbers this week: 2, 14, 15, 25.

14–20 OCTOBER 2000

Your organizational skills will come in handy this week because of the absence of a superior. If giving orders, make certain that you do so in a friendly manner; an overbearing attitude will work against you and you will find no co-operation when it is most needed. Do not try to go it alone; you need all the help you can muster.

Your lucky numbers this week: 1, 15, 26, 36.

21–27 OCTOBER 2000

Seek knowledge that would be helpful to your creative work. This is a good week for anything that does not require a great deal of co-operation from outsiders. Much of value can be learned by visiting a library, museum or similar place of learning. At the end of the week an unexpected health problem could lead you to cancel a social happening planned for the weekend.

Your lucky numbers this week: 1, 2, 26, 34.

28 OCTOBER–3 NOVEMBER 2000

Make an effort to contact people who could be of special help when it comes to furthering your career. If you have your mind set on a creative field, remember that it is essential to make the best possible use of personal introductions. People who matter are likely to favour you this week, and you should have no difficulty projecting your personality in a likeable manner. A recent investment should begin paying off now.

Your lucky numbers this week: 2, 25, 26, 32.

4–10 NOVEMBER 2000

After the events of last week, you should be able to look back with satisfaction. Bear in mind that this is not a particularly good time for matters of the heart. You could waste valuable time if you chase rainbows. Stick with matters connected to work. Accept invitations to social gatherings where you have an opportunity to rub shoulders with the rich and the influential.

Your lucky numbers this week: 14, 15, 26, 31.

11–17 NOVEMBER 2000

You may not be thinking straight about money. It would be extremely dangerous to make new investments now. Expert advice comes at little cost and could eliminate the possibility of losing out if you go your own way. New business propositions must be carefully investigated, and be wary about getting too deeply involved with people you meet for the first time. Try to avoid becoming overly emotional.

Your lucky numbers this week: 5, 16, 26, 30.

18–24 NOVEMBER 2000

Speculation could still be your downfall. The temptation to invest in the propositions suggested by friends will be very strong. Keep your impulses in check. It is wise to look before you leap. At times of uncertainty, consult your partner for advice. Single Snakes will find a romantic period this week.

Your lucky numbers this week: 2, 3, 5, 29.

25 NOVEMBER–1 DECEMBER 2000

Opposition to your plans from your partner will be difficult to comprehend. The actions of loved ones may appear totally illogical. It would be best to avoid family disputes with people who are acting impulsively. This is an ideal week for dealing with the basics of work and business. Deal with priorities, and rise straight to the top. Romance will be exciting. Someone you date for the first time is likely to turn out to be more than a ship that passes in the night.

Your lucky numbers this week: 14, 15, 26, 31.

2–8 DECEMBER 2000

You may have to alter your plans for this week in order to avoid serious arguments. Although you might feel that people are behaving irrationally, they will be calling the tune. Co-operation will be difficult to obtain, but this is a good week for jobs that offer you the chance to display your artistic prowess, especially if you can do so alone.

Your lucky numbers this week: 1, 3, 26, 34.

9–15 DECEMBER 2000

Use brain rather than brawn this week. Extra money can be earned through increased mental activity rather than physical energy. Creative enterprises can be made more valuable if you join forces with people who have specialist knowledge that you appear to lack. There will be no need to go it alone. This is an excellent week for teamwork on any level.

Your lucky numbers this week: 2, 3, 23, 29.

16–22 DECEMBER 2000

Travel should be postponed this week. This is not a good period for making long journeys, either for business of pleasure. If you cannot avoid it, then be particularly cautious if driving. Take no risks on the road. Be sure to check your car before you leave, especially your tyre pressure.

Your lucky numbers this week: 1, 26, 27, 30.

23–29 DECEMBER 2000

An extremely happy week for activities in and around the home. There will be great opportunities for improvements in your relationship with your partner. Differences that have been glossed over can now be discussed to everybody's benefit. An engagement this week is likely to lead to a happy marriage.

Your lucky numbers this week: 5, 15, 26, 36.

30 DECEMBER 2000–5 JANUARY 2001

You will have difficulty in understanding the impulsive actions of loved ones and plans you were keen to carry out in connection with your home may not be acceptable to them. It is also possible that someone is trying to deceive you. Work matters will be relatively simple compared to the domestic situation. This is a good week for experimenting with your working methods.

Your lucky numbers this week: 14, 15, 26, 27.

6–12 JANUARY 2001

It is quite likely that the problems of loved ones will interfere with your plans. A member of your family may not be feeling too well, so it might be necessary to cancel reservations. Do not be too disappointed if long-planned entertainment activities have to be postponed at the last minute at the weekend.

Your lucky numbers this week: 10, 25, 26, 31.

13–19 JANUARY 2001

If you can keep impulsive tendencies in check, this will be a good week for business. You must keep an eye on your extravagant streak. If you play your cards right, you could raise your earnings considerably in the not too distant future. A more romantic week than usual will be awaiting you.

Your lucky numbers this week: 1, 24, 26, 32.

20–26 JANUARY 2001 (24 JANUARY: CHINESE NEW YEAR – YEAR OF THE SNAKE)

No one and nothing can interfere with your plans for this week. This will be a most enjoyable week, when you can do exactly as you please. Home and work pressures ought to be reduced considerably. Trips and visits will be successful, especially if you are visiting friends or relatives you have not seen for some time. They will be happy to see you.

Your lucky numbers this week: 4, 15, 26, 33.

THE SIGN OF THE
Horse

The Chinese name for the Horse: Ma
The seventh sign in the Chinese zodiac
The hours governed by the Horse: 11am–1 pm
The corresponding sign in the Western zodiac: Leo
Element: Fire
The direction of the pole: Positive

*

The Year of the Horse in the Western Calendar

25 January 1906–12 February 1907 Fire Horse
11 February 1918–31 January 1919 Earth Horse
30 January 1930–16 February 1931 Metal Horse
15 February 1942–4 February 1943 Water Horse
3 February 1954–23 January 1955 Wood Horse
21 January 1966–8 February 1967 Fire Horse
7 February 1978–27 January 1979 Earth Horse
27 January 1990–14 February 1991 Metal Horse
12 February 2002–31 January 2003 Water Horse

Famous People Born Under the Sign of the Horse

Neil Armstrong, Rowan Atkinson, Samuel Beckett, Ingmar Bergman, Leonard Bernstein, Leonid Brezhnev, Eric Cantona, Frédéric Chopin, Sean Connery, Kevin Costner, Cindy Crawford, James Dean, Clint Eastwood, Thomas Alva Edison, Britt Ekland, Linda Evans, Ella Fitzgerald, Harrison Ford, Bob Geldof, Billy Graham, Gene Hackman, Rita Hayworth, Jimmy Hendrix, Janet Jackson, Nikita Khrushchev, Vladimir Ilych Lenin, Paul McCartney, Nelson Mandela, Rembrandt, Anwar Sadat, Helmut Schmidt, Lord Snowdon, Barbra Streisand, Raquel Welch, John Travolta, Mike Tyson, Antonio Vivaldi, Robert Wagner, Andy Williams, Michael York.

The Horse in a Nutshell

POSITIVE QUALITIES
You are diligent, enterprising, ambitious, friendly and humorous, with a sharp tongue.

NEGATIVE QUALITIES
Restless, impatient, rebellious, self-occupied and rather moody.

CAREER SUGGESTIONS
You will be an excellent politician, athlete or salesperson and will succeed in any kind of work where you can make use of your own initiative and powers of persuasion.

Main Features of the Horse

You are hardworking and effective in your work, and ambitious and a go-getter in your everyday life. You tend to possess endurance but lack patience.

LUCK
You are blessed with good fortune, and are optimistic and earthy. You will go far in life. At the same time you are very curious, and like to deal with matters involving competition.

MONEY

You will make good money in any kind of business involved with competition. Especially, you can be a good speculator in money games.

WORK

You like to make extra effort with your work, and meet any kind of competition with great courage. You could be a banker or broker or any kind of professional dealing with money transactions.

SOCIAL LIFE

You are fond of people and thrive in others' company. You especially like to be at the centre of the lives of your loved ones.

BUSINESS

You are effective and active. If you see a possibility, you do not let it go. In other words, a good businessman.

LOVE

You are elegant and stylish, but in love you tend to jump from one person to the other. This might create problems for you, but you will always have luck and get what you want.

PARENTS

You have very considerate, caring parents, though you might be a little spoilt by them.

SISTERS AND BROTHERS

You have wonderful sisters and brothers who are willing to support you. There is much love between you, and your lives will be prosperous.

CHILDREN

You are fond of children, but at times you think it is too much work. Among other things they might slow down your own development in the desired direction.

TRAVEL

You are the biggest adventurer in the Chinese zodiac. Travel to foreign places is a passion and a joy for you. Throughout your life you will travel around, never stopping in one place for a long period of time.

HEALTH

You have very good health. No one can beat you there. You love sports and thrive on being outdoors. You are fond of trees and the countryside. You want to roam around, just like a wild Horse.

INVESTMENTS

No one is better than you at speculating and seeing the best opportunities. You are a moneymaker for people around you, and you will never go in need of a penny.

TALENTS

You are enterprising and ambitious. Your willingness to assist others can help you go far. But you must learn to be patient and take one step at a time rather than racing through life at a gallop.

PROSPECTS

If you learn to be more patient and take one step at a time, then you will sooner or later get what you want in life. In other words – you are a winner.

What Kind of Horse Are You?

THE WOOD HORSE 1954, 2014

This the Horse in the skies. You are sociable and fond of life. Quick-witted and effective, you are always willing to give a helping hand to people around you; this makes you very popular among friends.

THE FIRE HORSE 1906, 1966

This is a Horse in motion. You are very adventurous, always on the go. You are fond of challenges and always search for excitement. Your life will never be dull, but you will have to take a break every now and then.

THE EARTH HORSE 1918, 1978

The Earth Horse is the most caring and considering type of all. You are service-minded and honest. You prefer to think before you leap.

THE METAL HORSE 1930, 1990

This it the family Horse. You are sharp-minded and effective in what you do. You may be a little restless, but sooner or later you come into contact with influential forces that carry you forward. In other words, a very lucky Horse.

THE WATER HORSE 1942, 2002

This is the Horse used by the military, a real fighter. You can go far, and enjoy the trust and image you have made for yourself. There will be some strenuous years in your youth, but you will become very influential when you get older.

The Ascendants of the Horse

11PM–1AM: THE HOUR OF THE RAT 'ZI'

This combination is rather difficult, because the Rat will never love the Horse, so you might get yourself into trouble if you are careless. You will also have to watch out for your impulsiveness and impatience, as otherwise the Rat and the Horse will be riding together into the dark.

1AM–3AM: THE HOUR OF THE OX 'ZHOU'

This is a very interesting combination, in which the Ox is slow and self-confident, while the Horse is impulsive and seeking success. If they can agree on the division of labour, with these two strong animals you will undeniably hold winning cards in whatever you choose to do.

3AM–5AM: THE HOUR OF THE TIGER 'YIN'

You are very energetic and impulsive, with the two of the strongest animals in you, combining elegance with opportunism, luck with lively intelligence. Your life will never be dull, but you need to take break in between adventures.

5AM–7AM: THE HOUR OF THE RABBIT 'MAO'

You are a wise dandy, combining elegance and ardour with highly developed moral demands which can sometimes conflict with your pride. Your charm is irresistible. Though you could at times be very bad-tempered, you will be forgiven in most circumstances.

7AM–9AM: THE HOUR OF THE DRAGON 'ZHEN'

Thirsty for voyage and adventure, this combination makes you very impatient and impulsive. People around you might envy your natural brilliance and elegance. You will be eloquent, an effective orator and a natural leader. At the same time you will attract honours and prestige, and your life will never be dull.

9AM–11AM: THE HOUR OF THE SNAKE 'SI'

With the Snake in you, you tend to be a bad loser and do not accept failure. You are a winner and will not hesitate to be opportunistic and sly. Since you are irresistibly charming, you will go far in your efforts to stay on top.

11AM–1PM: THE HOUR OF THE HORSE 'WU'

With this combination you are destined for success. You are an impetuous and ardent animal, a combination that gives you elegance with opportunism, luck with lively intelligence. You may just learn about that rare flower called modesty, but even then you must be careful not to trample on it.

1PM–3PM: THE HOUR OF THE GOAT 'WEI'

This Horse appreciates the arts and the good life. You are cultured and enjoy the company of friends in the upper classes. You will need an epic life; your ardour will be conquering, but you will prefer art and heroic poetry to warlike expeditions. In other words, you are a natural artist where you can enjoy success in new fields.

3PM–5PM: THE HOUR OF THE MONKEY 'SHEN'

You are eloquent and courageous. Your path will resemble an extended race course, from which the Horse/Monkey can only emerge victorious. Uniting intelligence with a fine appearance, you exploit to the utmost your resources of charm, talent, willingness and – sometimes – deceit.

5PM–7PM: THE HOUR OF THE ROOSTER 'YU'

Distinguished, loyal and generous, you are also at times very indecisive. Sometimes you like to stand out from the crowd and dominate; sometimes you prefer to control from behind. These two kinds of behaviour can be very strenuous and at times destructive.

7PM–9PM: THE HOUR OF THE DOG 'XU'

You are loyal and faithful. You tenaciously make your way by day and night, prodded by your intuition. You succeed in controlling both your pride and your fear of failure, never hesitating to smile at your own defects and weaknesses, yet you remain ardent and passionate. You are truly a reliable working Horse.

9 PM–11 PM: THE HOUR OF THE PIG 'HAI'
Blessed with a broad and clear intelligence, this combination is well aware of the pride that eats away at you. You have a tendency to overrate the true value of your possessions and conquests, and overlook their impermanence. Your ardour and impulsiveness often give way to doubt and mystery, but in the end you will succeed.

The Year Ahead

The Horse is the most noble of man's conquests. Allied to the power of the Horse, man overcomes distance and appropriates wide-open spaces. In the Chinese zodiac, the Horse has a fine reputation. Proud in appearance, for centuries he has been the friend of man, carrying him into the heat of battle or enjoying with him the delights of country retreats.

People born under this sign are essentially gregarious. You love the social life and crave acceptance. Agreeable companions, glib and eloquent talkers, you know how to please and enjoy it. Never modest, you are popular and adept at attracting attention.

The childhood and youth of the Horse will be critical. You will leave your family when young. Forced to assert yourself early in life, you will meet difficulties. You will suffer emotionally and financially, often having to sell out in order to start a new project. In maturity you will achieve calm and equilibrium, for you will have learned the wisdom of failure and the value of perseverance. Your old age will be serene.

The female Horse is passionate and lives according to the rhythms of her heart, which may sometimes get carried away so that her entire physical being will be affected deeply. You are sentimental, impatient and avid for love, seeking to conquer as much as you hope you can. You love immediate attractions and falling in love at first sight – a smile, a look, and there you are, in love.

As the Horse, you are very realistic and pragmatic, though not self-seeking. Once you are financially independent, you are content and ask for nothing more. You are lucky with money. Life with you is exciting and adventurous.

This will be a good year for the Horse, especially if you are dealing in investments. Your life will continue just as smoothly as last year. You can expect good news or even an increase in your family in this fine period. You are riding high on the waves of an earlier stage, and here you will achieve success. Furthermore, you are optimistic and have great faith in yourself. This is good for your surroundings. On a personal level, you are also going through a fast-moving stage. All you have to do is to take care of all these opportunities and get things done.

Week By Week For People Born Under the Sign of the Horse

5–11 FEBRUARY 2000 (5 FEBRUARY: CHINESE NEW YEAR – YEAR OF THE DRAGON)

The start of the year will be very interesting, but you will have to be diplomatic and meet people halfway. Try to find compromises wherever you can. You will not get very far if you try to do things alone this week. This is the right time to think about the future, so attend to matters concerning security when you are old. Invest in your own future rather than splashing out on goods of temporary value.

Your lucky numbers this week: 1, 12, 23, 34.

12–18 FEBRUARY 2000

An excellent period for anything connected with romance. You are clearly able to let your partner know how you feel concerning just about any aspect of life and you have more than enough nerve to carry out an audacious personal plan. When you need support, you should find that it is ready and waiting in the wings. This is a period for action.

Your lucky numbers this week: 4, 15, 26, 34.

19–25 FEBRUARY 2000

This is another hectic week. Make sure that you know what is expected of you. Nobody can tell you how to behave at the moment, though it may seem that is what most individuals are doing. A new perspective on an old problem can help you out no end by the weekend.

Your lucky numbers this week: 1, 2, 18, 30.

26 FEBRUARY–3 MARCH 2000

Do not be shy about thinking big because it is possible that your most grandiose schemes may work out this week. The reaction of people is extraordinary, leading you to believe that you can get away with almost anything that you conjure up.

Your lucky numbers this week: 3, 23, 28, 30.

4–10 MARCH 2000

Things are still looking good, though practical concerns maybe seem less urgent as the weekend approaches. You should turn your attention to your personal life, which looks more exciting than it has done for sometime. Remove any obstacles from your personal path with haste.

Your lucky numbers this week: 1, 14, 26, 32.

11–17 MARCH 2000

Deep thoughts provide new perceptions on many personal matters. This does not prevent you from being yourself and from doing what comes naturally, at work and socially. You might fancy a change of scene after work and can probably spend some time with a special person.

Your lucky numbers this week: 1, 2, 23, 34.

18–24 MARCH 2000

Family and domestic matters now use up most of your time, leaving little room for advancing your career. Patience is required, though you might find it hard to locate it within yourself just at the moment. Experience and common sense are important in most situations right now.

Your lucky numbers this week: 2, 15, 25, 36.

25–31 MARCH 2000

The domestic sphere of life continues to take up much of your energy. You may be planning to spend more time with your nearest and dearest this week. Meanwhile you need to tidy up various practical activities now so that you can continue with them next week in a more positive manner.

Your lucky numbers this week: 5, 12, 18, 30.

1 April–7 April 2000

You should now have more time to devote to the more practical aspects of life. You are even able to turn difficult situations to your own advantage. It is only a matter of time before you find an answer to a difficult problem and you will be able to do some thinking to help out a friend.

Your lucky numbers this week: 4, 5, 15, 36.

8–14 April 2000

The emphasis this week seems to be on pleasure. There will probably be little time to deal with practical considerations that this period might demand of you. Keep an eye on finances, which are probably not very healthy at the moment. It will not be long before they improve though, at the end of the week.

Your lucky numbers this week: 9, 12, 18, 31.

15–21 April 2000

Helpful and heart-warming news is on the way; it probably comes from a good friend abroad. The advantage of this is that you can take what is being said and use it as a platform for your own ideas. The creation of more space for yourself is also on the agenda for what should be a positive week.

Your lucky numbers this week: 15, 12, 18, 32.

22–28 April 2000

Things are bound to be quieter at the beginning of the week, but this is only temporary. Both energy and time are scarce, so it would make sense to find effective ways and means of using both.

Your lucky numbers this week: 6, 12, 18, 30.

29 April–5 May 2000

You can make good use of invitations, whether at work or in your social life. You cannot decline such offers. Although it seems some time off, you may already have your sights on your hopes for the summer. A very interseting trip will be in store.

Your lucky numbers this week: 5, 12, 18, 31.

6–12 May 2000

With potentially exciting things happening in all areas of life this week, nothing can prevent you from being cheerful and positive in your general approach. Not everyone is inclined to agree with you, but you have the powers of persuasion to bring almost anyone round to your side this week.

Your lucky numbers this week: 1, 4, 18, 36.

13–19 MAY 2000

Work and career projects create certain pressures that you would rather do without. Remaining calm and relaxed under most circumstances, however, you will learn how the slight irritations of the week can bring a new perspective. Not everyone around you turns out to be equally helpful.

Your lucky numbers this week: 5, 19, 28, 34.

20–26 MAY

You need to develop your capacity for self-expression, and there are reasons to believe that this is what you discover this week. No matter what the weather is doing outside, it is a time of sunshine and showers. Even when difficulties arise, Horses will have the capacity to deal with them in no time at all.

Your lucky numbers this week: 1, 12, 18, 31.

27 MAY–2 JUNE 2000

An excellent time for getting away from it all. This probably means that for once you become something of a hermit, which will certainly not suit everyone you come across at present. A slow but steady pace gradually leads to an exciting event waiting around the corner.

Your lucky numbers this week: 4, 6, 10, 16.

3–9 JUNE 2000

Co-operation is the keynote now. This is a splendid period for reaching an agreement with your partner on the best way to handle joint affairs. It is also a good time to begin work on your home; start those painting and redecorating jobs. Anything that gives you an opportunity to be artistic will have a special appeal for you this week. Speculation could bring you luck for a change. This is a week for travel and for dealing with long-distance affairs.

Your lucky numbers this week: 1, 12, 18, 34.

10–16 JUNE 2000

If you can control your impulsive nature, this will be a good week for business. You must watch your extravagant streak. You may suddenly feel like spending wildly but articles you are tempted to buy will be luxuries without great practical use. Worthwhile agreements can be consummated with people in senior positions. If you play your cards right, you could increase your earnings considerably in the not too distant future. People will generally be helpful and sympathetic to your wishes.

Your lucky numbers this week: 1, 12, 18, 32.

17–23 JUNE 2000

Work will tend to be strenuous. You will have some difficulty in keeping up the schedule this week, and it will be hard to promote teamwork. You must rely on yourself more than usual. You are good with words, but the gift of the gab may desert you. Health continues to require more attention than usual. A week where you have to fare cautiously.

Your lucky numbers this week: 2, 3, 6, 21.

24–30 JUNE 2000

No one and nothing may interfere with your plans for this week. This will be one of those enjoyable times when you can do exactly as you please. Pressures at home and work ought to be reduced considerably. Get out and about more, and if you feel you have been falling into a rut, take some positive action to alleviate the tedium. Trips will be successful, especially if you are seeing friends or relatives you have not visited for some time.

Your lucky numbers this week: 15, 18, 22, 34.

1 JULY–7 JULY 2000

Chances are you will be feeling rather edgy this week. You will find it difficult to settle down to any job for very long. The additional demands and impulsive actions of members of your family will not help matters. Distant affairs continue to be rather confused. Sudden, unexpected events could disrupt plans for a journey in connection with your business interests.

Your lucky numbers this week: 3, 12, 28, 30.

8–14 JULY 2000

Meet people halfway and look for compromise solutions wherever you can. You will make little progress if you try to go it alone this week. This is the right time to consider the future. Take out an insurance policy if you do not have one or you feel that you need more coverage. Pay attention to matters connected with security later in life.

Your lucky numbers this week: 5, 12, 18, 36.

15–21 JULY 2000

This is a perfect week for travel and drumming up support in new areas. You will find it easy to be congenial with influential people you meet for the first time. Horses seeking new positions at work may well be lucky and find tailor-made roles.

Your lucky numbers this week: 1, 11, 18, 30.

22–28 JULY 2000

Stay out of the public eye. Secret agreements could pay off, and it is important not to let too many people in on what you are currently negotiating. You can be inclined to gossip, but you must keep quiet to protect your own interests. Trust nobody with information that you have been told not to share. The mail is important this week. Business correspondence should not be neglected.

Your lucky numbers this week: 15, 17, 19, 33.

29 JULY–4 AUGUST 2000

You could be in a fidgety mood in this rather slow, dull week. Don't be tempted to act impulsively. Accept the fact that nothing of any great significance is going to take place. Housewives born under this sign will feel cut off and isolated if trapped at home for any length of time. Not a very favourable week for dealing with influential people. Wait for better opportunities.

Your lucky numbers this week: 1, 4, 5, 10.

5–11 AUGUST 2000

People will be unco-operative. It will be difficult to work out why superiors are refusing to back your ideas. It may be rather boring, but it would be in your very best interests to focus on routine matters. It is unlikely that you will make any money from speculative ventures right now.

Your lucky numbers this week: 1, 4, 5, 30.

12–18 AUGUST 2000

Relatives will be overly sensitive. Be sure that your sharp tongue does not get you into hot water. What you say could easily be read the wrong way by an older member of your family who has been feeling unwell of late. Avoid emotional scenes at all costs. This is a good week for work requiring mental agility.

Your lucky numbers this week: 2, 5, 18, 29.

19–25 AUGUST 2000

Use your imagination. Focus on work that gives you an opportunity to make full use of your artistic flair. Avoid your superiors. Influential people will be contrary and reluctant to grant favours. If you are trying to drum up support travel will not be helpful.

Your lucky numbers this week: 1, 4, 8, 35.

26 AUGUST–1 SEPTEMBER 2000

Although you may visualize all sorts of idealistic concepts, you may be striving for impractical goals. Home life needs a more commonsense approach. Arguments within the household may be unavoidable but they may serve as a prelude to sorting out your domestic problems. Even new plans now being made are likely to dissolve completely.

Your lucky numbers this week: 1, 12, 18, 33.

2–8 SEPTEMBER 2000

Another slow week when you have to be on your guard against deceptive influences. Marital difficulties have to be faced. You and your partner will have problems in reaching a compromise. It will be difficult to overcome differences where trust has been damaged. Money lies at the root of your problems at the moment.

Your lucky numbers this week: 2, 3, 14, 30.

9–15 SEPTEMBER 2000

Pay as much attention as possible to creative work. Do not neglect your natural talents. It might be possible to make some spare cash by brushing up on skills that have become rusty. Take up a hobby that once meant a great deal to you but may have been neglected because of pressure from your work. In other words, a very creative week, where you have the chance to be constructive.

Your lucky numbers this week: 1, 12, 18, 35.

16–22 SEPTEMBER 2000

Continue your effort to get a creative job off the ground. There should be few disturbing influences to slow you down. Money can be earned by focusing more attention on hobbies and second-string jobs than by slaving with your career. A very good week for contacting influential people.

Your lucky numbers this week: 1, 22, 23, 25.

23–29 SEPTEMBER 2000

You are in the middle of a generally favourable period. Be sure to exploit the excellent opportunities presenting themselves to you now. This will be a fairly slow, quiet week, but good openings lay the foundation for changes you wish to make in the near future.

Your lucky numbers this week: 1, 2, 18, 36.

30 SEPTEMBER–6 OCTOBER 2000

It will be easier to get along with members of your family. If you are married, you should be able to deal with differences with your spouse. Try to become involved in activities where your partner can be more involved. Co-operative work will bring you closer together and trips will be pleasant. This week is also the most outstanding period for single Horses. Romantic matters will bring greater happiness than they have for a while.

Your lucky numbers this week: 1, 12, 18, 33.

7–13 OCTOBER 2000

Go easy with money. Think carefully before investing in anything that could jeopardize your resources. Risks are unlikely to pay off and creative projects must be kept in check. Do not develop your plans just because a superior has verbally promised support. Bring yourself down from the clouds.

Your lucky numbers this week: 2, 3, 25, 36.

14–20 OCTOBER 2000

There will be a good opportunity to explain your point of view. Take advantage of the chance you get to address a large group of people whose support could be valuable. An excellent week for travel and handling all matters pertaining to distant affairs. Your creative flair will be much in demand.

Your lucky numbers this week: 1, 4, 15, 26.

21–27 OCTOBER 2000

The health of a loved one could cause you some concern. More of your spare time will have to be devoted to looking after others. Personal activities or a project you have been hoping to promote will have to be postponed. You will not find it easy to make any sacrifices at the end of the week.

Your lucky numbers this week: 2, 13, 23, 26.

28 OCTOBER–3 NOVEMBER 2000

You may be feeling a bit uneasy and at a loss what to do. Recent events have probably left you rather drained. It would be an idea to pay attention to personal health matters, especially diet. No important business transaction should take place this week. Matters under discussion ought to be left until after you have some time to think things over.

Your lucky numbers this week: 11, 12, 18, 35.

4–10 NOVEMBER 2000

Control your temper. Now you are inclined to jump to conclusions too quickly. This tendency could harm your career, especially if you are working with business contacts. Allow more give and take in your professional relationships. Otherwise, the week is good for romance.

Your lucky numbers this week: 3, 14, 15, 26.

11–17 NOVEMBER 2000

Your mind will be on matters taking place far away. You may have to do some travelling. It will certainly be difficult to stay away from what is taking place in other cities. Useful agreements can be consummated so do not hold out for exorbitant terms. You could lose a useful contract if you price yourself out of the market.

Your lucky numbers this week: 4, 5, 16, 36.

18–24 NOVEMBER 2000

Be prepared for a slow and uneventful week. As long as you can adapt to the steady pace you will have no problems. If you try to force things, however, you will probably wear yourself to a frazzle without achieving anything of permanent value. Devote your attention to health problems. As the business scene is rather quiet, this is a ideal time to pay attention to minor ailments.

Your lucky numbers this week: 4, 5, 7, 30.

25 NOVEMBER–1 DECEMBER 2000

Be ready for anything. It may be rather difficult to stick to the schedule you have made for this week. Loved ones will be unpredictable; their extra demands could make you miss an important appointment in the middle of the week. Matters with business have to be taken seriously.

Your lucky numbers this week: 2, 3, 15, 35.

2–8 DECEMBER 2000

Let someone else take centre stage. This will be a look, listen and learn period. What you learn will probably be interesting. It is possible to pick up a great deal from others' performances. Influential people will be impressed by your calm manner, so show you can keep your head while others around you are losing theirs. Do not be pressured into signing any documents.

Your lucky numbers this week: 11, 26, 27, 30.

9–15 DECEMBER 2000

Be first; beat your competitors to the punch. Get off to an early start. This will be a good week for Horses who immerse themselves totally in work. Relatives will be congenial. If there are problems to cope with at home, you should find that an older family member is willing to stand in for you.

Your lucky numbers this week: 5, 12, 18, 36.

16–22 DECEMBER 2000

The lack of distractions should make it possible to deal with work that demands intense concentration. It would be silly to waste your time attempting to start something fresh. Projects you have in mind need far more work before they are ready to be shown to people who could offer valuable support. Take one step at a time: you will succeed.

Your lucky numbers this week: 1, 2, 6, 17.

23–29 DECEMBER 2000

Use this week to iron out the differences that arose recently between you and your boss. Your charm will help you to develop stronger associations with people you will undoubtedly need to rely upon in one way or another. This will be a good weekend to build up the relationships with influential people around you.

Your lucky numbers this week: 1, 2, 15, 16.

30 DECEMBER–5 JANUARY 2001

If you are able to hold your impulsive tendencies in check, this will be a good week for business. You will have to play your cards right, so your earnings will increase in the not too distant future. People will generally be helpful and sympathetic to your aims.

Your lucky numbers this week: 6, 7, 18, 29.

6–12 JANUARY 2001

So long as you minimize financial outgoings, this can be a quite satisfactory week. A word of warning: do not buy off people you feel could help you. Wining and dining with expensive lunches will not bring what you want in your career. Influential people will be more co-operative if they feel you are prepared to pull your full weight.

Your lucky numbers this week: 10, 27, 28, 30.

13–19 JANUARY 2001

You might find certain people un-responsive to your point of view at present, but you should be able to achieve a great deal on your own so it really does not matter too much. A refreshing change in personal circumstances makes you more cheerful than ever. It brightens up the weekend.

Your lucky numbers this week: 2, 3, 18, 29.

20–26 JANUARY 2001 (24 JANUARY: CHINESE NEW YEAR – YEAR OF THE SNAKE)

A most rewarding phase comes along, even if this does not manifest itself in any particularly dynamic way just for the moment. It is the undertones of life that offer you the most, and that it is why it is sensible to keep your ear to the ground. Meanwhile enjoy the very best of what your social life offers you.

Your lucky numbers this week: 1, 26, 27, 30.

THE SIGN OF THE
Goat

The Chinese name for the Goat: Yang
The eighth sign in the Chinese zodiac
The hours governed by the Goat: 1pm–3pm
The corresponding sign in the Western zodiac: Cancer
Element: Earth
The direction of the pole: Negative

*

The Year of the Goat in the Western Calendar

13 February 1907–1 February 1908 Fire Goat
1 February 1919–19 February 1920 Earth Goat
17 February 1931–5 February 1932 Metal Goat
5 February 1943–24 January 1944 Water Goat
24 January 1955–11 February 1956 Wood Goat
9 February 1967–29 January 1968 Fire Goat
28 January 1979–15 February 1980 Earth Goat
15 February 1991–3 February 1992 Metal Goat
1 February 2003–21 January 2004 Water Goat

Famous People Born Under the Sign of the Goat

Pamela Anderson, Jane Austen, Anne Bancroft, Boris Becker, George Burns, Andrew Carnegie, Leslie Caron, Lord Carrington, Catherine Deneuve, Robert De Niro, John Denver, Douglas Fairbanks, Margot Fonteyn, Paul Gascoigne, Bill Gates, Mel Gibson, Mikhail Gorbachev, George Harrison, Julio Iglesias, Franz Kafka, Buster Keaton, Mick Jagger, John Major, Michelangelo, Benito Mussolini, Sir Laurence Olivier, Norman Tebbit, Rudolph Valentino, Vangelis, Terry Venables, Lech Wałesa, George Wallace, John Wayne, Bruce Willis, Debra Winger, Boris Yeltsin.

The Goat in a Nutshell

POSITIVE QUALITIES
Imaginative, friendly, peaceful, flexible, and possessing artistic talents.

NEGATIVE QUALITIES
Moody, pessimistic, a little rigid and tending to be very insecure.

CAREER SUGGESTIONS
Nurse, doctor, priest, social worker, politician or artist, or any kind of profession where you can make use of your creative mind.

Main Features of the Goat

You are gentle and caring, and may be a little uncertain about yourself. In some ways you tend to lose yourself in your own dreams.

LUCK
As long as you manage to avoid unnecessary worries and let your self-assurance come forward, then luck and prosperity will smile on you.

MONEY
You have prospects of inheriting money from your family, but you could also make money through your own efforts if you want to. You will not go short.

WORK

You could be a doctor or nurse or do anything dealing with people, just to be able to give the care and attention you often like doing. A very service-minded person, in other words.

SOCIAL LIFE

You are fond of people and any kind of gathering. Many will think you are crazy about throwing parties because you cannot stand to be alone.

BUSINESS

You are smart in business and understand the art of dealing with people around you. If you have the right support, then you will go far in anything to do with business.

LOVE

You are well regarded and popular, but be careful that too many people do not come knocking at your door at the same time. Something like this will create quite a mess for you.

PARENTS

Your parents are understanding and love you dearly. You prefer to have a very good relationship with your mother; you adore her.

SISTERS AND BROTHERS

You have a solid and sound relationship with your siblings. You are often the eldest one in the family, so that your sense of parenthood will play an important role. You like to be father or mother to your loved ones.

CHILDREN

You are very fond of children and know quite well what you would like to do for them. They adore you as a caring and attentive parent.

TRAVEL

You like travelling, but try to stick to places where you have been before. Your cautious nature helps you avoid problems.

HEALTH

You are physically very strong, but you have a very delicate and vulnerable body that you need to take care of.

INVESTMENTS

You possess a strong sense of judgement and know how to invest money wisely. Many of your friends tend to ask you for advice.

TALENTS

You are gentle and considerate. You love looking after those around you. You like to help people but at times you can be too self-sacrificing. You would be wise to respect your own needs as well as those of others.

PROSPECTS

As long as you feel peace and quietness around you you will thrive and prosper. The worst thing for you is to discuss and quarrel unnecessarily. You are seeking a world without conflict.

What Kind of Goat Are You?

THE WOOD GOAT 1955, 2015

This is a cultivated and well-mannered Goat. You know your limits and are satisfied with what you manage to acquire in life. You will enjoy harmony and happiness in whatever you choose to do.

THE FIRE GOAT 1907, 1967

This is a Goat who has lost his way, one that has great happiness in addition to many unnecessary worries. Life is exciting, but if you want to get by you will have to make certain efforts.

THE EARTH GOAT 1919, 1979

This is the mountain Goat, active and full of energy. Try to slow down a little; you go too fast. Many people are willing to support you, in any circumstances. You will lead a happy and harmonious life.

THE METAL GOAT 1931, 1991

This is a Goat with many inner resources. You are kind and tolerant. You will have to take many serious decisions when you are young, but things will improve when you settle down with a partner who is more than willing to support you.

THE WATER GOAT 1943, 2003

This is a Goat who prefers to stay in the crowd. You are quick-minded and effective, and you prefer to work in a team. At times you can be rather naïve, so you will have to be careful not to be exploited by others.

The Ascendants of the Goat

11PM–1AM: THE HOUR OF THE RAT 'ZI'

This is an excellent combination for the Goat, who responds to the very different charm and wit of the Rat. Both will have a tendency to float about in a world of illusions, but as they will get something worthwhile out of it, it does not matter if they seem blind or deaf; for these two it can be a useful way of dealing with the world.

1AM–3AM: THE HOUR OF THE OX 'ZHOU'

This could be a somewhat difficult combination. The Goat wants to take it easy, while the Ox in you wants to work hard and take life seriously. These two extremes sometimes mean that you experience a real fight within yourself. But if you can let one animal at a time dominate, then things will work out all right.

3AM–5AM: THE HOUR OF THE TIGER 'YIN'

This is a Goat with great energy, who knows what he wants. A strong fighter with soft claws, he will only be difficult if you provoke him. If you take him seriously, though, he will be a gentle and peaceful Goat.

5AM–7AM: THE HOUR OF THE RABBIT 'MAO'

You are a dreamer with this special combination. If you cannot find the comfort which is so dear to you, you will seek it in your fantasies. You love travel, and are always seeking some-thing even more marvellous. You have a supple nature and are intuitive and charming. Life will be good to you.

7AM–9AM: THE HOUR OF THE DRAGON 'ZHEN'

You are very idealistic and possess great artistic talent. You differ greatly from other types of Goat in that you always complete any tasks you set yourself. You are also more organized and ambitious.

9AM–11AM: THE HOUR OF THE SNAKE 'SI'

This combination makes for a very thoughtful Goat indeed. You possess great wisdom and knowledge that you put to good use. But it is dangerous to fall in love with you – and you are skilled in the art of seduction. This kind of Goat will enjoy great luck and have the advantage of good taste and a capacity for finesse.

11AM–1PM: THE HOUR OF THE HORSE 'WU'

You are the Goat who is always on the go, not just physically, but also mentally. You are creative with many bright ideas, but when you are unable to realize them you have a tendency to escape into a fantasy world. People around you might regard you as a dreamer.

1PM–3PM: THE HOUR OF THE GOAT 'WEI'

Your sense of reality will be precarious, which does not bother you in the least. With this combination, you will love travel and be ever ready to leap about and cavort. Though your road is littered with traps, you will never be discouraged, taking it all with good will, humour and a free and easy manner.

3PM–5PM: THE HOUR OF THE MONKEY 'SHEN'

You are intuitive and intelligent, and at the same time extremely restless. The Monkey likes to leap from branch to branch, and the Goat leaps ceaselessly from cloud to cloud. This alliance will be particularly lively and eventful. You can be a real heartbreaker in love.

5PM–7PM: THE HOUR OF THE ROOSTER 'YU'

Sometimes you set yourself too many goals that are impossible to reach. Although you are generous and out-going, you are also often unreliable and difficult to pin down. You have the tendency to kick out and back away. You will not accept ties, advice or any form of dependency.

7PM–9PM: THE HOUR OF THE DOG 'XU'

Your intuition is just remarkable, but you tend to make things complicated. You are forever changing your moods, ideas and decisions and constantly retracing your steps and becoming distrustful and pessimistic. At times you are aggressive and indecisive – in other words, a very difficult person to be with.

9pm–11pm: the Hour of the Pig 'Hai'

You are a very sentimental and self-sacrificing Goat, almost a bit too nice and naïve. However, you can also be very stubborn and proud. You are slow to recognize your errors, though this does not stop you from being tolerant and ready to forgive.

The Year Ahead

As the Goat, you are stubborn and difficult to understand, but you are also intuitive, motherly and self-sacrificing. Your childhood is a delicate time for the Goat, and is influenced by the relative harmony and security of your family. Your youth will be marked by uncertain and emotional behaviour – at times inconstant and hesitant – amounting to instability. On the other hand you will be lucky during maturity, and in old age you will be contented and want for nothing.

You are creative, imaginative and ingenious. All those who are born under this sign want to devote their free time to the arts, which to them are tantamount to a religion. In practical matters you need someone to take charge of administration, letting you develop your creative talents. Goats need money, but you prefer not to have to earn it. The best solution is to find someone who is well organized and has the money to support you.

The female Goat has a special gift for creating an agreeable ambience around you, which contributes to your social standing. You are even faithful, as long as you are not abused and your partner dedicates himself to you exclusively, or, in return for your fidelity, you can expect something that you value. A little flirtation here and there, for your own amusement and to verify your seductive powers, will suffice. You always know how to save yourself for special occasions.

The year 2000 will be calm and constructive for those born under the sign of the Goat. You will enjoy a very successful period, especially where work is concerned. You have a tendency to be too careful and timid, so make a real effort to grasp opportunities – no one can do it for you. After a time of uncertainty regarding love, the clouds will begin to clear now. The summer is especially favourable for romance. An encounter with an old flame could develop into something special, so do not let this chance pass if you are single.

Week By Week For People Born Under the Sign of the Goat

5–11 FEBRUARY 2000 (5 FEBRUARY: CHINESE NEW YEAR – YEAR OF THE DRAGON)

You find it easier to get along with members of your family. Married Goats should be able to overcome problems with their spouses. Try to involve yourself more in activities where your partner can take an active role – co-operative work will help to bring you closer together. Trips to far-off places will be rewarding this week.

Your lucky numbers this week: 1, 13, 19, 30.

12–18 FEBRUARY 2000

Important long-term plans made this week will affect your whole family. Consultations with partners will ease the burden somewhat. This is not a good week for visiting friends or relatives; your presence will not be welcome and will cause unease. Keep financial expenditure to a minimum.

Your lucky numbers this week: 12, 13, 24, 36.

19–25 FEBRUARY 2000

Goats who handle heavy or complicated machinery should make certain that equipment operates satisfactorily; accidents are likely through no fault of your own. At home, have electrical apparatus checked over before use. Romance suffers from the intervention of a third party.

Your lucky numbers this week: 2, 11, 13, 30.

26 FEBRUARY–3 MARCH 2000

Rewards, though not necessarily financial ones, will be gained by those willing to go out of their way on behalf of a colleague. A relationship exists between you and a worker of the opposite sex; do not jeopardize this by trying to put it on a romantic level.

Your lucky numbers this week: 1, 13, 19, 31.

4–10 March 2000

In-laws cause many problems this week. Discourage them as best as you can, though confrontations are inevitable. Family squabbles will be the rule rather than the exception, unfortunately. Finances take a battering this weekend because of foolish purchases.

Your lucky numbers this week: 2, 3, 21, 34.

11–17 March 2000

Those working around the home are advised to take all safety precautions as accidents are likely. It is quite possible that you will suffer sprains and strains, in some cases even minor breaks. Be very careful. Friends dropping in at the end of the week can be commandeered into helping.

Your lucky numbers this week: 1, 11, 19, 34.

18–24 March 2000

Try not to miss opportunities that arise at work this week. You may well be looking the wrong way when something important happens. This week you must put yourself in the right place at the right time. Financial matters take a turn for the better, especially where speculative ventures are concerned.

Your lucky numbers this week: 11, 13, 19, 32.

25–31 March 2000

Complete outstanding work early in the week before launching into new projects. Travellers will find that delays beyond their control will bring losses and disappointment. There is also a danger you may contract a chill or a cold while travelling. An elderly relative may give cause for alarm this weekend.

Your lucky numbers this week: 1, 3, 10, 33.

1 April–7 April 2000

Guard against mishaps at home this week. If tradespeople are working for you, watch what they are doing. Breakages and losses could be caused through their carefree attitudes. This weekend will see your romantic life taking a turn for the better. Even married Goats will feel their hearts fluttering.

Your lucky numbers this week: 12, 13, 19, 36.

8–14 April 2000

Others around you seem moody and pessimistic. Do not let them put a damper on your own personal plans. If necessary, leave them at home while venturing forth. Drivers are warned of the possibility of car breakdowns and malfunctions. Check out your vehicle to avoid this.

Your lucky numbers this week: 9, 13, 19, 31.

15–21 APRIL 2000

Those dealing with property could be in for some setbacks late this week. Try to sort things out at the beginning of the week. Documents relating to property should be left for signature in another week. Financial losses resulting from wild speculative ventures are also indicated. Do not get involved with the schemes of colleagues.

Your lucky numbers this week: 11, 13, 19, 36.

22–28 APRIL 2000

Arrangements for the future could be made this week, but it is unlikely that they will succeed. Keep an eye open with regard to promises being made, especially with those of a romantic nature. A partner is trying to deceive you. Home entertaining appeals to you this weekend, but it could turn out to be very expensive.

Your lucky numbers this week: 1, 2, 19, 37.

29 APRIL–5 MAY 2000

You can usually take most things in your stride – but not this week. You will be easily thrown by the smallest upset, and there are plenty of those around at present. A chaotic period is about to begin concerning your work and social life.

Your lucky numbers this week: 11, 13, 19, 33.

6–12 MAY 2000

You will have to make a choice this week. Do you look forwards or backwards to solve a work problem? The only way to find out is through discussion with a partner. Financial matters are not a problem this week so you can afford to spend a little on yourself in order to give your ego a much needed boost.

Your lucky numbers this week: 11, 13, 19, 32.

13–19 MAY 2000

You will probably not get much done this week because of the problems of a brother or sister. Try and give all the help you can without attaching strings to your favours. This week it will be your turn to approach someone for advice. Do not be too proud to seek solutions from someone younger than yourself.

Your lucky numbers this week: 10, 13, 19, 35.

20–26 MAY 2000

Changes around you have little effect, but you will hardly be able to go through the week without acknowledging that something is going on. Colleagues are edgy. Superiors are likely to withdraw support from a pet project, much to your relief. Children are a source of amusement and pleasure.

Your lucky numbers this week: 1, 13, 19, 27.

27 MAY–2 JUNE 2000

Your mood is one of quiet optimism. Problems at home are receding and your working scene is decidedly rosy. Do not be lulled into a false sense of security. Something will come out of the woodwork and hit you between the eyes. Remain vigilant for the unexpected.

Your lucky numbers this week: 4, 13, 19, 32.

3–9 JUNE 2000

Money you have been expecting fails to arrive. You get yourself deeper in debt. Try not to spend more than you have. Romantic partners feel restless and you will have to use all your charm to stop them wandering away from the straight and narrow.

Your lucky numbers this week: 12, 13, 19, 32.

10–16 JUNE 2000

Golden opportunities come your way but you are going to miss out on them unless you are ready to grab. Do not make false economies. It will be worth going further into the red to get what you really want from your work. This weekend is excellent for romance for young people.

Your lucky numbers this week: 1, 18, 19, 33.

17–23 JUNE 2000

Financial rewards for previous work come your way this week, putting you back in credit. A good week for consultations with bank managers and accountants. Be warned against doorstep salesmen trying to sell below-average products. Do not be tempted to buy anything you do not really need.

Your lucky numbers this week: 8, 13, 19, 34.

24–30 JUNE 2000

You will be feeling in need of a rest, so do not involve yourself in energetic pastimes. Goats involved in physically taxing sports will find themselves unable to keep up with others. This weekend should be put aside for rest and relaxation, and is a good time for getting together with a friend of the opposite sex. It promises to be a very romantic and erotic encounter.

Your lucky numbers this week: 1, 13, 19, 31.

1 JULY–7 JULY 2000

It will be all too easy for you to give offence this week, especially when dealing with your seniors. Bite your tongue. This weekend is a good time for getting together with a romantic partner, and married Goats should find great excitement in the company of their spouses.

Your lucky numbers this week: 3, 15, 18, 36.

8–14 JULY 2000

Do not try to work too hastily – instead, take things as they come. Colleagues are not co-operative, so you will not be able to seek favours from them. You may have to work longer hours than usual, but you should enjoy the mental stimulation this provides.

Your lucky numbers this week: 1, 13, 19, 31.

15–21 JULY 2000

Do not let uncertainty be your bedfellow this week. Even if you feel a little uncertain about yourself, keep this from others. Hide your true feelings from all those who could exploit them. Loved ones should be an exception to this rule, as they are in need of love and assurance.

Your lucky numbers this week: 1, 18, 20, 36.

22–28 JULY 2000

A very good week for romance. It is likely that Mr or Miss Right could be working quite close to you without you realizing it. Look around; romance may be found on your doorstep – literally. If you take a shine to the friend of a friend, you will have to be very careful how you handle the situation.

Your lucky numbers this week: 1, 2, 13, 35.

29 JULY–4 AUGUST 2000

This week will not be all you expected. Plans made some time ago for social events this week will go wrong. All travel arrangements should be checked. Work will continue as usual, but you will have to take one step at a time.

Your lucky numbers this week: 5, 13, 14, 25.

5–11 AUGUST 2000

This looks like being a very dull week at work. No progress can be made and you are possibly considering a new and more challenging form of employment. Be warned – this is not the time to make changes. Your social life picks up this weekend with an invitation from an unexpected source.

Your lucky numbers this week: 11, 13, 19, 32.

12–18 AUGUST 2000

Financial difficulties lead you into consultations with your bank manager. Begging letters will achieve nothing. Be honest about your problems and you will get a sympathetic hearing – and possibly some assistance. This is a good week for romance, however; new partnerships will be entered into, and these could be longlasting.

Your lucky numbers this week: 11, 12, 23, 34.

19–25 AUGUST 2000

Do not be tempted out and about with friends. Their company invites problems. Better by far that you stay and catch up with chores around the house. Some home improvements will not go amiss. You will be able to lose yourself in whatever you turn your hand to.

Your lucky numbers this week: 17, 28, 29, 30.

26 AUGUST–1 SEPTEMBER 2000

Younger members of the staff brighten up what threatens to be a dull week. Finances receive a boost because of a shrewd investment paying dividends. In-laws could cause you problems on the domestic front if you allow them to influence your partner. Children are a source of irritation this weekend.

Your lucky numbers this week: 1, 13, 19, 31.

2–8 SEPTEMBER 2000

This is a socially eventful week, when invitations arrive like snowflakes; be wise and only accept those where you know you will have fun. It is time to forget the politics of work and get down to enjoying yourself. Those involved in the entertainment industry will receive some bad news from a partner.

Your lucky numbers this week: 5, 26, 27, 29.

9–15 SEPTEMBER 2000

Take advantage of any bargains offered on shopping sprees this week. An extremely good purchase will be made. Unexpected news in the mail from someone living a long way off will start you thinking about moving.

Your lucky numbers this week: 1, 13, 21, 22.

16–22 SEPTEMBER 2000

A busy end to the working month, and a week that is both interesting and eventful. It might seem on occasions that too many people are expressing their points of view at the same time, which can make your head spin. This is an ideal item for reaching a sensible agreement.

Your lucky numbers this week: 5, 13, 19, 36.

23–29 SEPTEMBER 2000

High spirits return this week. You should feel capable of handling almost anything, especially in professional matters. Personal attachments are rewarding, but you need to consider the feelings of someone sensitive, possibly a friend, who could have been paying too much attention to a negative comment.

Your lucky numbers this week: 19, 31, 32, 36.

30 SEPTEMBER–6 OCTOBER 2000

Your sensitivity is particularly acute at the moment, perhaps too much for your own good. Known friends and respected colleagues are the people you should be mixing with, though there may be an isolationist quality in the air, which can make you feel lonely. It may be difficult to act boldly.

Your lucky numbers this week: 11, 13, 18, 30.

7–13 OCTOBER 2000

Now is a good time to put new plans into action. You could notice a favourable interlude in business matters. All social engagements also bring out the best in you; in fact it would not be going too far to suggest that your popularity is at its height.

Your lucky numbers this week: 4, 13, 19, 32.

14–20 OCTOBER 2000

Issues can be rather complicated this week, and you may not be willing to consider them sensibly. You could always stand back for a while and wait to see how things transpire before taking major decisions.

Your lucky numbers this week: 11, 12, 19, 36.

21–27 OCTOBER 2000

Concentrating on essential tasks can be very boring, which is one of the reasons why you will need to ring in changes if you can this week. Goats are not very good at dealing with routine, and change is your hallmark. More interesting times are at hand. Wait patiently.

Your lucky numbers this week: 1, 13, 14, 25.

28 OCTOBER–3 NOVEMBER 2000

This week you display the resolve to succeed. Practical projects receive your full attention while changes can be made to improve the general circumstances within your life. Powerful emotions are in evidence and that means you are speaking your mind romantically.

Your lucky numbers this week: 11, 17, 19, 36.

4–10 NOVEMBER 2000

The best way to deal with people who may not have been on your wavelength recently is to talk to them carefully. Although you have spoken carefully, voicing your opinions at present need not create particular problems. All in all, it's what the world expects of you.

Your lucky numbers this week: 11, 13, 19, 32.

11–17 NOVEMBER 2000

This week use almost any means at your disposal to get what you personally want from life. You take others with you on a magical journey, even if this trip is only in your mind. Your renewed magnetism is particularly evident at present, and this would be a good time for getting what you really want.

Your lucky numbers this week: 2, 9, 10, 30.

18–24 NOVEMBER 2000

Stay away from the intrigues of others, even though you may not be able to avoid involvement in family disputes. It really is important to remain as impartial as you can, partly because you are busy with other things at the moment too.

Your lucky numbers this week: 5, 13, 19, 30.

25 NOVEMBER–1 DECEMBER 2000

Outside influences stimulate your overall imagination, and matters requiring a careful, logical approach can prove testing. Interesting diversions fill all your spare time and the more creative side of your nature begins to have greater control. Intuition and instinct prove the best guides.

Your lucky numbers this week: 11, 14, 20, 32.

2–8 DECEMBER 2000

A breath of fresh air blows through your life as the general atmosphere keeps improving, particularly with regard to romantic and leisure pursuits. You will now have a chance to let off steam in the company of people you care for the most. People of importance are willing to let you to have your way.

Your lucky numbers this week: 1, 13, 19, 34.

9–15 DECEMBER 2000

You could not be accused of taking other people for granted this week, though perhaps you are not paying as much attention as you could to your own needs and wants. On a personal level, arguments are likely, especially if you consider that others are casting doubt on your opinions.

Your lucky numbers this week: 1, 13, 19, 31.

16–22 DECEMBER 2000

New possibilities arise and social invitations beckon. All encounters with groups or associations can be turned to your advantage and would certainly help to make life a little lighter or more carefree. A positive attitude towards work can bring great benefits for you at present.

Your lucky numbers this week: 2, 3, 11, 34.

23–29 DECEMBER 2000

Changes now bring an excellent and light-hearted influence into your life. Within this week you find yourself on the receiving end of news, some of which comes from far away. Pay attention to any messages and be prepared to back your hunches for a while.

Your lucky numbers this week: 12, 13, 19, 35.

30 DECEMBER–5 JANUARY 2001

Your chart gets stronger and stronger, making romance more of a probability than you may have expected. Single Goats may observe more opportunities in romance, though all of you can expect more consideration from your loved ones and a helpful attitude, especially from surprising directions.

Your lucky numbers this week: 1, 14, 19, 31.

6–12 JANUARY 2001

Tension strikes home in emotional issues. At this stage you are likely to keep loved ones at bay, and should not allow yourself to be too cut off. Channel all your energies into important short-term plans, leaving more adventurous schemes until the new week gets started.

Your lucky numbers this week: 2, 15, 19, 36.

13–19 JANUARY 2001

Look out at pleasant social encounters; you should find yourself talking to one or two people whom you really like. Your instincts are good, as they will be all week, and you won't go far wrong if you trust in any new relationship. The building blocks of life seem to be in your own hands.

Your lucky numbers this week: 1, 13, 20, 31.

20–26 JANUARY 2001 (24 JANUARY: CHINESE NEW YEAR – YEAR OF THE SNAKE)

This week may prove to be the best time of the month to complete outstanding duties and obligations before you start examining fresh fields and pastures new. There can be setbacks, with others appearing reluctant to put themselves out for you. You simply have to make allowance for that fact.

Your lucky numbers this week: 3, 12, 19, 36.

THE SIGN OF THE
Monkey

The Chinese name for the Monkey: Hau
The ninth sign in the Chinese zodiac
The hours governed by the Monkey: 3pm–5pm
The corresponding sign in the Western zodiac: Gemini
Element: Earth
The direction of the pole: Positive

*

The Year of the Monkey in the Western Calendar

2 February 1908–21 January 1909 Earth Monkey
20 February 1920–7 February 1921 Metal Monkey
6 February 1932–25 January 1933 Water Monkey
25 January 1944–12 February 1945 Wood Monkey
12 February 1956–30 January 1957 Fire Monkey
30 January 1968–16 February 1969 Earth Monkey
16 February 1980–4 February 1981 Metal Monkey
4 February 1992–22 January 1993 Water Monkey
22 January 2004–8 January 2005 Wood Monkey

Famous People Born Under the Sign of the Monkey

David Bellamy, Jacqueline Bisset, Björn Borg, Victor Borge, Yul Brynner, Julius Caesar, Princess Caroline of Monaco, Johnny Cash, Jacques Chirac, David Copperfield, Joan Crawford, Timothy Dalton, Charles Dickens, Ian Fleming, Paul Gauguin, Jerry Hall, Tom Hanks, Harry Houdini, Mick Jagger, Lyndon B. Johnson, Edward Kennedy, Leonardo Da Vinci, Walter Matthau, Peter O'Toole, Anthony Perkins, Lisa Marie Presley, Jevgenji Primakov, Debbie Reynolds, Eleanor Roosevelt, Diana Ross, Bertrand Russell, Paul Scofield, Tom Selleck, Omar Sharif, Martin Shaw, Rod Stewart, Elizabeth Taylor, Kiri Te Kanawa, Harry Truman, the Duchess of Windsor, Zhao Ziyang.

The Monkey in a Nutshell

POSITIVE QUALITIES
Imaginative, friendly, colourful, quick-witted, very intelligent and amusing in many ways.

NEGATIVE QUALITIES
Egotistic, sly and self-centred – at times so naughty and sly that you ultimately even trick yourself.

CAREER SUGGESTIONS
You are multi-talented and find any kind of profession suitable. With your gift of speech and intelligence you would be a great politician, salesman, writer or journalist.

Main Features of the Monkey

You are just super-intelligent and learn things very fast, but you lack endurance and tend to jump from one thing to another without scruple.

LUCK
Your great joy and happiness is to find someone who understands you and takes part in your activities.

MONEY

There will be great luck in your life, but you will have to apply the right amount of logic and Monkey intelligence to create this fortune.

WORK

You are a trouble-shooter, fit for any kind of work that demands quick thinking and creative solutions to problems.

SOCIAL LIFE

You are the most joyful sign in the Chinese zodiac. You are fond of people and appreciate speed and excitement.

BUSINESS

Born under this sign, you are the master of all trades and you know what you want. No matter what you do, you will be able to make money from everything you touch.

LOVE

You are romantic and fond of the opposite sex. Unfortunately you are not very faithful, and have the tendency to jump from one lover to another.

PARENTS

Your parents think that you are clever and exciting, but at times hard work, because you can get into trouble and need helping out.

SISTERS AND BROTHERS

You are a cunning diplomat, but you get on well with your loved ones, who find you exciting and loveable.

CHILDREN

You love children and like many in your life, but once you have them, you are so busy with other matters that you do not always have much time for them.

TRAVEL

You like travelling to unknown places as you are always curious and looking for excitement.

HEALTH

You are strong in body and mind, but tend to be on the go so much that you forget to take good care of yourself. Slow down a bit – you need it.

INVESTMENTS

You are good at investments and can get other people to take part in your projects. Sometimes you are too smart for your own good and can ultimately fool yourself.

TALENTS

You are very creative and versatile. Anything to do with communication and design may appeal greatly to you, and you could do well in these areas.

PROSPECTS

You can go far in life, but only if you play your hand of cards without cheating.

What Kind of Monkey Are You?

THE WOOD MONKEY 1944, 2004

This is the Monkey who lives up in the trees. You are clever and caring. When young, you must overcome many hindrances, but life will be easier later on. Under any circumstances you will succeed and lead a happy life.

THE EARTH MONKEY 1908, 1968

This is the Monkey from the mountains. You are clever and adventurous, and can never sit still. Your life is exciting, and you have a good business sense. You can become both rich and powerful.

THE METAL MONKEY 1920, 1980

This is a very independent Monkey, who is both restless and indecisive. You have to work hard in order to make ends meet, but you will have a wonderful and happy old age.

THE FIRE MONKEY 1920, 1992

This is the Monkey who lives in the fruit garden. You enjoy life, and could be restless but enterprising. It is written in the stars that you could become powerful and rich, but you are doomed to work hard, as you cannot keep still.

THE WATER MONKEY 1932, 1992

A clever and elegant Monkey, very intelligent and sociable, though you can change your mind easily. Try to stick to one thing at a time. You will have the possibility of marrying into a very rich family, thus obtaining fame and power.

The Ascendants of the Monkey

11PM–1AM: THE HOUR OF THE RAT 'ZI'

This is one of the most adventurous combinations in the Chinese zodiac. Before going on a trip, make sure that you have a first-aid kit with you. Your journey through life is more likely to be more like a hazardous adventure than an agreeable outing. The Monkey in you will be full of ideas and the Rat will use all his tricks, causing you to fall into physical, moral and even spiritual traps. The journey of life will be like a prize-fighting ring where all blows are allowed and no rules are observed.

1AM–3AM: THE HOUR OF THE OX 'ZHOU'

This combination is remarkably agile. Physically and mentally you are a first-rate acrobat, gifted with rare powers of persuasion. However, you must be careful, because the Monkey is sometimes a sorcerer capable of transforming the power of the Ox into mere confetti.

3AM–5AM: THE HOUR OF THE TIGER 'YIN'

Combining the ever present wizardry of the Monkey with the proud bearing and temperate skills of the Tiger, you are a formidable animal who can turn anything upside-down and provoke many a sleepless night. You are constantly on the go and should try not to get up to so many tricks at once.

5AM–7AM: THE HOUR OF THE RABBIT 'MAO'

You will be an inventive, lively and rather airy animal. You tend to be calculating, and leave nothing to chance. You prefer scheming, conjuring and scounging over hard, irksome work. With this combination, you envisage life as a game in which, for the fun of it, you adorn yourself with traps and mirages to zigzag between them.

7AM–9AM: THE HOUR OF THE DRAGON 'ZHEN'

Supremely gifted as well as possessing a talent and taste for walking the tightrope, as a valiant and fearless guardian you will never take off your armour. You are always prepared for war.

Your days and nights are spent in a state of alertness, much to the continued astonishment of your friends.

9AM–11AM: THE HOUR OF THE SNAKE 'SI'

This is not an easy combination. You are an intelligent and quick-witted creature but your tendency to get carried away will be tempered by deep reflection. Even so, you may well refuse to listen to the advice of others because of your own sense of pride and self-esteem.

11AM–1PM: THE HOUR OF THE HORSE 'WU'

With this combination you are both courageous and eloquent. Your path in life will resemble a lengthy race course, from which you can only emerge victorious. You will be as well balanced as a race horse, and get by uniting your resources of charm, talent, wiliness and, sometimes, deceit.

1PM–3PM: THE HOUR OF THE GOAT 'WEI'

You are a romantic Monkey with many tricks up your sleeve. At times pride will curb your fantasies and your ideas will then gain in constancy and consistency, though it is uncertain that you will want to pursue them to their logical end. The Monkey in you likes to jump from branch to branch, and the Goat leaps endlessly from cloud to cloud.

3PM–5PM: THE HOUR OF THE MONKEY 'SHEN'

You are by nature chivalrous, slightly boastful and often proud. You will find it difficult to stay on a straight course; in fact, you will be tempted to take detours and short cuts for the sheer pleasure of discovery and a taste for novelty. One thing is quite sure – you are super-intelligent.

5PM–7PM: THE HOUR OF THE ROOSTER 'YU'

Very proud of yourself, you will not be, to say the least, modest and self-effacing. You will make sure that you never go unnoticed and will care a great deal about your impact on others. Lacking neither intelligence nor good taste, you will be irresistibly attracted by all that glitters.

7PM–9PM: THE HOUR OF THE DOG 'XU'

Born in the hour of the Dog, you are a supremely intuitive Monkey. It will be difficult to put you off your trail; you will always find your way despite obstacles and difficulties. You have a tendency to complicate your life because you think of every-thing as a journey. You hate simplicity, straight lines and mapped-out routes.

9pm–11pm: the Hour of the Pig 'Hai'

This is a sporty and easy-going Monkey. The presence of the Pig in you makes you easy to approach, but you will always find it difficult to bargain as you are always too considerate towards the people you deal with.

The Year Ahead

The Monkey is very intelligent, but you can also be associated with dishonesty. Crafty, agile and clownish, the Monkey is a disconcerting animal who continues to surprise us, to baffle us. Skipping from branch to branch, you are restless, always moving to seek new excitement.

The infancy of the Monkey will be happy and pass without problems. You are intelligent, hard-working and adapt easily. Your youth, however, will be unstable, full of changes and emotional difficulties. In maturity, the Monkey will achieve tranquillity and success – but be careful in old age, when you will often be solitary and cut off from family and loved ones.

Women Monkeys behave with great charm and kindness, for they love to please and vaguely fear that they will not be liked. You are easily carried away, seducing others at the drop of a hat and throwing yourself into each new love with intensity. It is the temptation and conquest you are looking for, and you do not mind instantly following the first member of the opposite sex to pass.

This will be a good year for Monkeys. You are extremely strong and effective and will have an enormous need to make your mark this year. At the same time you have great luck and fortune in getting things done. You have a will of iron that nobody else can match during this period. New sides of your nature will surface. Your relationship will have many changes. It will be very intense and deep, and never before have you been so involved. This is the time for expansion; you will have the chance to grasp opportunities and get on with your success.

Week By Week For People Born Under the Sign of the Monkey

5–11 FEBRUARY 2000 (5 FEBRUARY: CHINESE NEW YEAR – YEAR OF THE DRAGON)

This week will be very promising. Keep certain plans or information up your sleeve, particularly regarding career matters. Others will be doing their best to try to seek out information, but as this is ultimately used to their own advantage – and certainly not yours – you need to be more secretive now.

Your lucky numbers this week: 1, 12, 15, 36.

12–18 FEBRUARY 2000

If you have been seeking favours from important people, now could be the best time to ask. You have more than a little cheek on your side, as well as the powers of persuasion to bring others round to your point of view. Most Monkeys should be feeling on the top of the world by the weekend.

Your lucky numbers this week: 3, 22, 25, 30.

19–25 FEBRUARY 2000

A positive and happy week can be expected, with social relationships especially bringing interest and diversity into your life. A slight element of caution is necessary as others may resent what they see to be your present lack of compromise. Any grudges should be abandoned immediately.

Your lucky numbers this week: 1, 12, 15, 31.

26 FEBRUARY–3 MARCH 2000

You are reaching both a physical and a mental peak. This should be especially marked in a professional sense, though this is not the only area of your life that benefits from current trends. The world stands waiting for you; all you have to do is to give the instructions.

Your lucky numbers this week: 4, 12, 15, 35.

4–10 MARCH 2000

This is the start of a lucky time, though you may not have time to notice since trends have been looking especially favourable for the last couple of days. A time to consolidate obvious gains and to make the most of social possibilities that recent days have offered.

Your lucky numbers this week: 1, 2, 15, 31.

11–17 MARCH 2000

Finances should strengthen quite noticeably at this time, allowing you to make more of any small risk you are willing to take. Although you may not be awash with cash at this time, you are able to make more of what is available and convince others to part with a little of their own wad.

Your lucky numbers this week: 9, 12, 19, 32.

18–24 MARCH 2000

You will not get anything free of charge this week; in other words, you will really have to work for whatever you want to obtain. However, things will ease up a bit from Wednesday onwards. The astrological aspects are very favourable for you from then on, and it seems likely that you will get what you want.

Your lucky numbers this week: 5, 16, 21, 27.

25–31 MARCH 2000

Everyone has to do things that go against the grain sometimes. This includes Monkeys as well, even though you might sometimes think that it should not. Deal with such jobs early in the week and leave yourself more time later to do whatever takes your fancy socially. Routine is certain to depress you.

Your lucky numbers this week: 11, 12, 15, 32.

1 APRIL–7 APRIL 2000

Impatience has to be negotiated with at the moment, as you probably began to realize last week. The trouble is that almost everyone you come across seems determined to be stupid. Of course your own actions lie beyond criticism – or at least that is what you try to convince yourself.

Your lucky numbers this week: 2, 22, 25, 35.

8–14 APRIL 2000

Happier trends can be expected in personal matters. Don't be surprised if it happens that everyone is suddenly behaving in a more rational and sensible way. I wonder if this has anything to do with the fact that they just happen to agree with your own distinctive point of view?

Your lucky numbers this week: 1, 12, 15, 31.

15–21 APRIL 2000

Much mileage from good ideas is possible. What a pity that you cannot do everything that you would wish at the moment, though if this turned out to be the case, you could not possibly have enough energy to get you through the day. Some projects will have to wait until later.

Your lucky numbers this week: 1, 2, 19, 36.

22–28 APRIL 2000

Curiosity is part of the magic of this week. Looking around with a sense of awe and wonder, you want to take everything to pieces in order to find out how it works. This is really not possible and it would make far more sense to simply accept that some things are the way that they are. Just appreciate them.

Your lucky numbers this week: 2, 18, 19, 34.

29 APRIL–5 MAY 2000

Your partner may get the upper hand this week; if you are a single Monkey, then it may be friends who seem to get the better of you. The real truth is that most people have your best interests at heart and will only be good to you if you allow them the chance and the time to prove the fact.

Your lucky numbers this week: 1, 12, 17, 35.

6–12 MAY 2000

The more expansive your attitude, the broader are the potentials that lie ahead. The outcome of this key week depends very much upon your own willingness to abandon routine tasks and adopt a more fluid attitude. Stay away from committees of any sort and show the world how much you know about everything.

Your lucky numbers this week: 10, 12, 15, 32.

13–19 MAY 2000

Any moves in your career at present need to be thought out very carefully, else you could find yourself getting in a little hot water further down the line. Not the most energetic week you will ever live through, though it's amazing what you can get done from your own armchair.

Your lucky numbers this week: 1, 19, 20, 31.

20–26 MAY 2000

Close relationships look especially good and bring you into a world of excitement and anticipation. There are times at present when the possibility of events turns out to be more exciting than the reality. Keep an open mind and remain optimistic.

Your lucky numbers this week: 11, 12, 15, 35.

27 MAY–2 JUNE 2000

An excellent week for expressing your personality to the full; it's a case of notifying the world in advance that you are coming. Most of the people you meet would be more than happy to hear your opinions but they may not come round to your thinking immediately. Some persuasion is necessary.

Your lucky numbers this week: 10, 13, 15, 32.

3–9 JUNE 2000

One obstacle after another could come along this week, but it all really depends on whether you insist on banging your head against a wall. If you notice the slight difficulties that are in evidence, you should also be able to change direction quickly enough. If everything seems fraught – go back to bed!

Your lucky numbers this week: 9, 12, 15, 34.

10–16 JUNE 2000

Your curiosity reveals itself again, so remember what happened to the cat that allowed this quality to get out of control. In reality you are safe enough, but you may discover that not everyone is keen to have you hanging around asking questions all the time. They may teach you some new words!

Your lucky numbers this week: 1, 12, 15, 31.

17–23 JUNE 2000

Your actions may attract more responsibility than you would realistically want to deal with this week. It might be best to mind your own business and make the most of diversions that demand nothing more than your interest and attention. Your creative potential is strong.

Your lucky numbers this week: 4, 12, 25, 36.

24–30 JUNE 2000

You have little choice but to slow things down a little. In all probability this is not something that you will have to worry about, since life will take this responsibility on your behalf. Delay new plans, though only for a day or two. Meanwhile, have a good rest.

Your lucky numbers this week: 11, 12, 15, 32.

1 JULY–7 JULY 2000

Obligations to other people start out being something of a drag. Fortunately this does not last long and before the end of the week you should discover that you are very happy to help almost anyone out. Not a time to creep around quietly or pretend that you are less capable than you really are.

Your lucky numbers this week: 11, 12, 17, 28.

8–14 JULY 2000

You may now be in for some good fortune, even if some of it is totally unexpected and may have actually gone by before you realize it. Give and take are important in personal relationships; you have plenty to keep you occupied.

Your lucky numbers this week: 11, 12, 15, 35.

15–21 JULY 2000

Opt for a change of scene this week, probably in active planning for what the week has in store for you. Getting to grips with jobs that have to be completed before Saturday might not be all that easy, especially since people involved seem unwilling or unable to help you along.

Your lucky numbers this week: 11, 22, 25, 36.

22–28 JULY 2000

You are in position of great influence when it comes to guiding others along a sensible path. What is really interesting is that you are able to help yourself on the way and to make new financial possibilities work in directions that you truly desire.

Your lucky numbers this week: 2, 25, 29, 30.

29 JULY–4 AUGUST 2000

Personal relationships are back in the forefront of your life, possibly because this week gives you the time that you need to concentrate on them. An age-old problem crops up, but you are in the right position and in the most positive frame of mind to deal with matters as and when they arise.

Your lucky numbers this week: 1, 12, 15, 36.

5–11 AUGUST 2000

The end of a particularly worrying situation that has been bothering you for some time is in sight. Now is the time to make long-term plans affecting your family. Relatives will be in need of some help and it is up to you to choose the most deserving. Romance is likely to be found within your working environment. Be bold and you will get what you want.

Your lucky numbers this week: 11, 12, 15, 32.

12–18 AUGUST 2000

A legal matter or family problem will be settled this week and you could benefit from its resolution. Be discreet when dealing with members of the opposite sex; you could land yourself in hot water through no fault of your own. Single Monkeys are in danger of being deceived romantically.

Your lucky numbers this week: 13, 22, 33, 34.

19–25 AUGUST 2000

You may wish for a quiet week, but this is not to be. You will be inundated with invitations from friends and relatives alike, and will have to sift through them carefully in order to decide which to accept – a good guide will be the state of your own particular finances.

Your lucky numbers this week: 1, 12, 15, 36.

26 AUGUST–1 SEPTEMBER 2000

What happens to other people around you this week will have a direct bearing on your own fortunes. Romantic problems will be cleared up in the middle of the week provided both parties are honest with each other. Deception will only make matters worse.

Your lucky numbers this week: 10, 12, 15, 32.

2–8 SEPTEMBER 2000

A week of good news, especially if you have been chasing a pay rise or a promotion. Rewards are also on the way for those who have persevered over the past months. The domestic situation gets better for married Monkeys; for single ones engagements may be possible.

Your lucky numbers this week: 9, 12, 15, 32.

9–15 SEPTEMBER 2000

Care and caution will pay off in all walks of life this week. Do not be too impulsive. Use tact and diplomacy when dealing with loved ones; they may rebel and then you can expect a minor revolution. You will need tact and diplomacy.

Your lucky numbers this week: 1, 12, 15, 33.

16–22 SEPTEMBER 2000

Travelling is uncomplicated and should be a pleasure this week. Those of you who stay at home will be rewarded by a spot of property improvement. This weekend should be spent with stimulating and exciting friends. Do not be afraid to spend some money on entertainment.

Your lucky numbers this week: 12, 23, 34, 36.

23–29 SEPTEMBER 2000

Do not let the opportunity for a romantic encounter pass you by this week, especially if you are ready to embark on a permanent affair. Married couples should spend this week together for maximum pleasure. The weekend will have to be devoted to an elderly relative who is not feeling well.

Your lucky numbers this week: 11, 12, 15, 30.

30 SEPTEMBER–6 OCTOBER 2000

Tensions at work will begin to fade away this week; you can look forward to a period of friendship and co-operation. Superiors who have withheld support for new schemes or projects will relent and you will be able to make a fresh start. New beginnings in your social life look set for this weekend.

Your lucky numbers this week: 10, 14, 19, 36.

7–13 OCTOBER 2000

A time for reflection. If you try to learn from past mistakes, you could move forward by leaps and bounds. Your energy level is high, so an extra-heavy workload will not bother you too much. Assistance can be requested from colleagues. Parents will be faced with unco-operative children at the weekend.

Your lucky numbers this week: 1, 12, 15, 34.

14–20 OCTOBER 2000

Now it is time to review your value system. It looks as though you have not been aiming sufficiently high with career matters. Have more confidence in yourself and your capabilities. Married

Monkeys will find that a new period of deeper understanding begins. The single Monkeys will be thinking of making a commitment.

Your lucky numbers this week: 11, 18, 19, 32.

21–27 OCTOBER 2000

A week for making a decision. You will have to put your trust in someone other than yourself. Work colleagues with problems to solve will ask for your advice. Give it only if you are sure of yourself; you might also give offence.

Your lucky numbers this week: 1, 13, 15, 34.

28 OCTOBER–3 NOVEMBER 2000

A financial windfall is indicated, although it looks as if wins on the roundabouts will be lost on the swings. You will have to take a more serious attitude to finances if you are to make any noticeable headway. Enlist family help should any heavy work be needed around the house.

Your lucky numbers this week: 2, 12, 19, 33.

4–10 NOVEMBER 2000

Some old things that happen within your working surroundings will leave you dumbfounded and somewhat frustrated. These events will work to your advantage as long as you are aware of what is going on. This weekend you should pay special attention to the advice of a member of the opposite sex.

Your lucky numbers this week: 1, 12, 15, 31.

11–17 NOVEMBER 2000

You may have a little more than usual to cope with this week because of the illness of an elderly relative. Do all you can to help, and try to keep the atmosphere free of panic. Travellers will have an exciting time this week, meeting new people and visiting new places. Total strangers will offer advice.

Your lucky numbers this week: 3, 10, 16, 36.

18–24 NOVEMBER 2000

Friends offer helpful advice on a career matter; colleagues will also steer you in the right direction. Promotion is in the pipeline for those who have been chasing it in the past few months. This weekend is a good time to meet colleagues socially. A minor family celebration is indicated.

Your lucky numbers this week: 11, 22, 25, 33.

25 November–1 December 2000

Proceed with confidence in everything you attempt, for you can hardly put a foot wrong. Push ahead with plans and ambitions, allowing no one to stand in your way. Superiors will be helpful in all aspects of your career. This weekend you should get together with friends and family.

Your lucky numbers this week: 1, 12, 31, 32.

2–8 December 2000

Things that come to light this week could set you thinking. If colleagues appear to be secretive, try to loosen their tongues. Charm, tact and diplomacy should do the trick. You may need to rebudget a family holiday plan – this could cause disappointment and delays to your plans.

Your lucky numbers this week: 11, 12, 15, 33.

9–15 December 2000

It appears that you have been rather hasty in condemning an old friend about something said. Try to make amends before it is too late. Friction may abound within your social life. If introduced to a new circle of friends, a club or association, be on your best behaviour in order to make the best impression. There is no need to spend cash to impress.

Your lucky numbers this week: 1, 22, 25, 32.

16–22 December 2000

Friends find it difficult to get through to you this week; you seem to have built a mental wall around yourself. This will need to be demolished if you wish to enjoy this week's events. Accept all invitations offered to you this weekend. Romantic encounters will be exciting and unusual.

Your lucky numbers this week: 11, 12, 15, 30.

23–29 December 2000

A whiff of money surrounds everything you do this week, so keep your eyes and ears open for the main opportunity. Speculative ventures should pay off, provided you are not too greedy. A concentrated push will be needed if you wish to launch new career plans. Enlist the help of colleagues.

Your lucky numbers this week: 1, 2, 15, 36.

30 DECEMBER–5 JANUARY 2001

Do not allow pessimistic work colleagues to put a damper on your spirits this week. You have everything going for you, and should make use of your ambitious aspirations. Travel offers the best dividends; commercial travellers and representatives should have an excellent time and profits will increase. Try to establish new business contacts within this field.

Your lucky numbers this week: 11, 12, 19, 33.

6–12 JANUARY 2001

A week when romance appears to control your every move. A member of the opposite sex catches your eye and you spend time daydreaming. Do something about it! Younger Monkeys could be swept off their feet by an older person, but do not take all the promises that are made to you that seriously.

Your lucky numbers this week: 3, 14, 15, 32.

13–19 JANUARY 2001

Check all your work thoroughly this week. You are likely to over-look something quite elementary that could cause you a few problems in the future. Communication is also quite important, especially telephone calls and letters at the weekend. Sign all documents that are of a legal nature to avoid disappointment.

Your lucky numbers this week: 1, 12, 19, 31.

20–26 JANUARY 2001 (24 JANUARY: CHINESE NEW YEAR – YEAR OF THE SNAKE)

The good things in life mean a great deal to you for the Monkey is rather materialistic. This makes you a lover of good food and drink, and this week is extra-favourable for parties and visits to gourmet restaurants. Emotionally you are fairly stable and prefer to stick yourself to your present partner.

Your lucky numbers this week: 11, 13, 15, 35.

THE SIGN OF THE
Rooster

The Chinese name for the Rooster: Ji
The tenth sign in the Chinese zodiac
The hours governed by the Rooster: 5pm–7pm
The corresponding sign in the Western zodiac: Taurus
Element: Earth
The direction of the pole: Negative

*

The Year of the Rooster in the Western Calendar

22 January 1909–9 February 1910 Earth Rooster
8 February 1921–27 January 1922 Metal Rooster
26 January 1933–13 February 1934 Water Rooster
13 February 1945–1 February 1946 Wood Rooster
31 January 1957–17 February 1958 Fire Rooster
17 February 1969–5 February 1970 Earth Rooster
5 February 1981–24 January 1982 Metal Rooster
23 January 1993–9 February 1994 Water Rooster
9 February 2005–28 January 2006 Wood Rooster

Famous People Born Under the Sign of the Rooster

Emperor Akihito, Francis Bacon, Severiano Ballesteros, Dirk Bogarde, Barbara Taylor Bradford, Michael Caine, Enrico Caruso, Eric Clapton, Grover Cleveland, Joan Collins, Rita Coolidge, Alexander Dubček, Mohamed Al-Fayed, Errol Flynn, Melanie Griffith, Alex Haley, Richard Harris, Goldie Hawn, Katharine Hepburn, Michael Heseltine, Elton John, Diane Keaton, Nancy Kerrigan, Dean Koontz, David Livingstone, Jayne Mansfield, Steve Martin, James Mason, Somerset Maugham, Bette Midler, Van Morrison, Willie Nelson, Kim Novak, Yoko Ono, Dolly Parton, Michelle Pfeiffer, Prince Phillip, Roman Polanski, Priscilla Presley, Nancy Reagan, George Segal, Peter Ustinov, Richard Wagner, Eddie Yang.

The Rooster in a Nutshell

POSITIVE QUALITIES
Faithful, generous, honest, caring and colourful, with many artistic talents.

NEGATIVE QUALITIES
Prickly, vain, conceited and very tactless.

CAREER SUGGESTIONS
You would be a good judge, policeman, politician, entrepreneur, reporter or artist, or even a well-known singer.

Main Features of the Rooster

You have a stable character and enough vision to follow what is happening around you. Your ideas and goals in life are very realistic; you are bound to go far with that attitude.

LUCK
You will usually be very lucky, because you will always get support and help from a colleague or friend around you.

MONEY

You can land yourself in trouble if you do not handle your financial matters in a proper way. You are very good at making money, but you have also the tendency of spending it away.

WORK

You like to be the boss and prefer to do things on your own.

SOCIAL LIFE

Your social life is active. You are fond of people and thrive when you have many things to attend to.

BUSINESS

Here you can apply your real talents; nothing really frightens you. Everything you do is effectively and thoroughly achieved. Even better, you are always very creative and find the right solutions to tasks you are faced with.

LOVE

You will meet the great love of your life and the relationship will prosper, though at times it might be hard work. You will have to demonstrate your feelings fully, so that everything can work out.

PARENTS

Your parents love you dearly. You appreciate their support and understanding.

SISTERS AND BROTHERS

Though you quarrel with your siblings, they will forgive you for being blunt. There is much love and harmony between you.

CHILDREN

You will have many children, though you prefer them to handle things themselves. You are convinced that it is better for them to make their own decisions.

TRAVELS

You will travel much and often, and these experiences will accompany you throughout your life.

HEALTH

You are strong, though tend to catch colds very easily, as your throat is the weak point of your body. Otherwise pay attention to your kidneys. If you are careful, nothing serious will happen to you.

INVESTMENTS

You can do what you like, because you know how to make money. Anything you touch will be turned to gold – though of course don't be too greedy.

TALENTS

You are ambitious and artistic, and you thrive in the limelight. However, you could also be a good lawyer if you decide to make use of your clever tongue.

PROSPECTS

You are persistent and smart in whatever you do. You can manage on your own, and serious problems will not force you to abandon your ideas.

What Kind of Rooster Are You?

THE WOOD ROOSTER 1945, 2005

You are the Rooster who likes to sing. You are straightforward, maybe talking or singing without having much to say. You will have a long and prosperous life. The relationship between you and your family will be good. Women Wood Roosters are home-loving.

THE FIRE ROOSTER 1957, 2017

You are the Rooster who seeks to do things in your own way. You are sensitive and sociable, and like to be acquainted with influential people. Your youth will be somewhat difficult, but your old age will enjoy security. Women Fire Roosters are talented, elegant and happy.

THE EARTH ROOSTER 1909, 1969

You are the Rooster that crows and shows the way. You will enjoy a good life, though family relationships will be troubled. You are clever and understanding. Children will come late in your life. Women Earth Roosters are thrifty and erratic.

THE METAL ROOSTER 1921, 1981

You are the Rooster who is born in a cage. You are both intelligent and active. You like to discuss, and people will respect your integrity. Women Metal Roosters are both talented and lucky.

THE WATER ROOSTER 1933, 1993

You are the Rooster who is born in the barn, and you are straightforward and righteous. You love gossip and cannot keep a secret. You will not receive any money from your family, so you will have to manage on your own. Throughout life you will be able to see new possibilities, and you will never be poor. Under any circumstances you will have a happy and harmonious old age.

The Ascendants of the Rooster

11PM–1AM: THE HOUR OF THE RAT 'ZI'

You are extra-intelligent and skilful, but at the same time tend to be very conceited. The Rooster in you is generous and has many ideas on how to use the money you make. Luckily the Rat in you is occupied with saving money. Maybe it is wise to get a job where you can use your talents with other people's money.

1AM–3AM: THE HOUR OF THE OX 'ZHOU'

You are energetic and take responsibility for what you do. You like to argue about almost everything before taking any action. You often apply your colourful rhetoric instead of your iron fists – a good combination of both the soldier and the priest.

3AM–5AM: THE HOUR OF THE TIGER 'YIN'

You possess a fascinating personality, with a trouble-shooter meeting someone who is quarrelsome and aggressive. You will not allow anyone to run away with anything unless you are being heard – and the others will probably have little choice. Luckily you are rather reasonable, as long as you do not feel provoked.

5AM–7AM: THE HOUR OF THE RABBIT 'MAO'

A quiet and efficient bird that can always find something to eat; you must always feel entitled to the right to oversee and control a situation and you feel you are the master of destiny. With this combination you are generous and lively and you have a pure heart, though you can be very indecisive at times.

7AM–9AM: THE HOUR OF THE DRAGON 'ZHEN'

A proud and imaginative Rooster, you possess the courage of the Dragon. Nothing is better for you than to be able to dominate, control and supervise in all circumstances. One thing is certain – no one will get bored with you around!

9AM–11AM: THE HOUR OF THE SNAKE 'SI'

An intuitive and frank animal, you will accomplish your tasks with a generous heart and much good will and honesty – compensating for the Snake's tendency to sidetrack – which will not prevent you from being uneasy. You will have a need to shine and surround yourself with costly and beautiful things; this may appear superficial, but it is vital for your sense of well-being.

11AM–1PM: THE HOUR OF THE HORSE 'WU'

Distinguished, loyal and generous, you are also very indecisive at times. Sometimes you like to stand out from the crowd and be dominant, at other times you prefer to control from behind the scenes. These kinds of behaviour can be very strenuous, and at times destructive.

1PM–3PM: THE HOUR OF THE GOAT 'WEI'

Sometimes you tend to set too many high-powered goals that are difficult to reach. Although you are generous and out-going, your character can prove unreliable and difficult to pin down. You have the tendency to kick out and back away, for you will not accept ties, advice or any form of dependency.

3PM–5PM: THE HOUR OF THE MONKEY 'SHEN'

Proud of yourself, you will not be modest or self-effacing. You will ensure that you never go unnoticed, and care greatly about the effects you produce on others. Lacking neither intelligence nor good taste, you will be irresistibly attracted by all that glitters.

5PM–7PM: THE HOUR OF THE ROOSTER 'YU'

This creature will not go by unnoticed. Others will turn to look at you, always dressed in the latest fashion, rather proud and trying to distinguish yourself among your companions. You dream constantly of being forever in the forefront. You are the symbol of vigilance, both protector and lookout, though you might be aggressive, susceptible, intolerant and rebellious if contradicted.

7pm–9pm: the Hour of the Dog 'Xu'

You are imbued with honour and fidelity. With this combination you will be a sentinel and guardian, yet capable of questioning your handsome self-assurance, looking into yourself and tempering your aggressiveness. You will make your way through good times and bad, straddling the two worlds of shade and sun. You will persevere, though without any desire for conquest or revenge.

9pm–11pm: the Hour of the Pig 'Hai'

With this combination you are a strange and solitary traveller. You stand out in a crowd, not so much with your appearance, but by your attitude towards life. In order to achieve this, you will seek a hiding place in which you can bury your treasures far from the eyes of the world.

The Year Ahead

The Rooster is above all a solar symbol, announcing the sun's rising with his morning song. It is also the emblem of the hero and of the guardian and protector of life – you can find it on top of many buildings. As the Rooster, you are always on the watch, looking down on men and scanning the horizon. In announcing daybreak you disperse ghosts and phantoms, the powers of illusion and darkness. You are the incarnation of the forces of youth, hope and clarity.

As the Rooster you will have problems during childhood, youth and maturity. Your life will be strewn with ups and downs. This will, however, teach you to understand the greatest joys and suffer the greatest sorrows. Sometimes you will be rich, sometimes poor. Occasionally you will find yourself surrounded by friends, at other times alone. But as soon as you attain emotional stability and become settled in a profession, your life will calm down. In any case, you will enjoy happy old age.

Women Roosters do not lack charm. Especially when you are young you attract a crowd of admirers, whom you lead by the nose. There is no need to worry about the future, for you are reasonable and will almost always choose someone both brilliant and capable to support the family you want to establish. You will adapt to married life with wisdom and humour. The woman Rooster is sociable, communicative and very active, and traditionally is not easy to live with, for you jealously protect your independence and refuse to allow any interference in your life.

Roosters can succeed in all professions demanding self-assurance, nerve and brilliance. Intelligent and skilful, you know how to convince and persuade others. Your taste for comfort and security encourages your desire for good pay and an appreciation of efficiency and practicality, but you dislike routine and prefer independence to subordinate positions. In any case you manage to get by. Your life is never dull, and if you can be more patient, you will become both rich and famous.

This will be a moderately good year, especially if you are not able to take care of what you have achieved in recent years, though it can also be very exciting, with many possibilities. To start risky investments this year is not recommended, and anything that promises fast money should be avoided. This is not the time to carry out any investment transactions. At this time you tend to make mistakes if you are not attentive. Minor power struggles involving you and your loved ones can also arise. Try to find a compromise with your partner. The last part of the year will be much better.

Week By Week For People Born Under the Sign of the Rooster

5–11 FEBRUARY 2000 (5 FEBRUARY: CHINESE NEW YEAR – YEAR OF THE DRAGON)

Many exciting and rewarding opportunities await you this year. Financial rewards are due for those Roosters who have put in some hard work over the past few weeks. You may have to push yourself forward this weekend in order to get your points across. Your opinions are worth listening to at present – make certain that other people hear your voice. This weekend is a very romantic time for all.

Your lucky numbers this week: 1, 12, 25, 32.

12–18 FEBRUARY 2000

Trouble with a partner could occur this week because of the presence of a third party in your entertainment plans. It would be best to go it alone and discourage friends from joining you. This is a good week for those wishing to catch up on odd jobs around the home, such as clearing out unwanted possessions.

Your lucky numbers this week: 11, 12, 15, 31.

19–25 FEBRUARY 2000

Travel is well aspected this week and long trips should be profitable and enjoyable. Shoppers will find bargains in new places. If you are involved in the travel industry, then you should have a very good week. Parents are advised to keep an eye on schoolchildren, who may have problems they are unwilling to discuss.

Your lucky numbers this week: 10, 12, 15, 33.

26 FEBRUARY–3 MARCH 2000

The sudden end to a work problem will take you by surprise and give an added boost to your career and financial status. Get routine work cleared up early on, as you will have important matters to face this weekend. Sign important documents, especially those connected with property.

Your lucky numbers this week: 1, 12, 15, 32.

4–10 MARCH 2000

A week to be positive. All your actions should be marked with a show of aggression. Let other people know what you are after. Superiors will be impressed by your aggressive attitude. Family problems that stem from ambitions for your career can be cleared up this week through consultation.

Your lucky numbers this week: 8, 11, 25, 35.

11–17 MARCH 2000

Those involved in the literary or artistic fields will have disappointing news in the mail. Do not be depressed by this; you must keep pushing forward. Financial rewards are higher than expected, especially bonus payments. This weekend is a good time for romance.

Your lucky numbers this week: 6, 12, 21, 36.

18–24 MARCH 2000

A week when you are likely to be oversensitive, which makes you vulnerable to the nastier elements at work. Try to ignore jibes and leg-pulling. Get on with business matters and ignore other people. This weekend will be happily spent in the company of those near and dear to you.

Your lucky numbers this week: 12, 15, 32, 36.

25–31 MARCH 2000

A very good week for romance. It is likely that Mr or Miss Right could be working quite close to you without you even realizing it. Look around you. Another place where romance may be found is on your doorstep – literally. If you take a shine to the friend of a friend, you will have to be very sensitive about how to handle the situation.

Your lucky numbers this week: 11, 22, 25, 30.

1 APRIL–7 APRIL 2000

This week will not be all that you expected. Plans made some time ago for social events this week will go wrong. All travel arrangements and places you wish to visit should be checked. Work will go on as usual, but you will have to take one step at a time.

Your lucky numbers this week: 1, 12, 15, 31.

8–14 APRIL 2000

This looks like being a very dull working week. No progress can be made and you are possibly considering a new and more challenging form of employment. Be warned – this is not the time to make changes. Your social life picks up this weekend with an invitation from an unexpected source.

Your lucky numbers this week: 5, 12, 15, 36.

15–21 APRIL 2000

Things look good, though are probably quieter towards the weekend. Now you should deal with matters of personal concern, which look more exciting than they have done for ages. Remove obstacles blocking your path as a matter of urgency.

Your lucky numbers this week: 10, 12, 15, 32.

22–28 APRIL 2000

You should now have more time to spend upon practical things and may even turn rather difficult situations to your own advantage. It is only a matter of time before you discover that a difficult problem is about to be solved. You will be happy to put your thinking cap on for the benefit of a friend.

Your lucky numbers this week: 21, 22, 25, 33.

29 APRIL–5 MAY 2000

Your energy is high this week and you cannot be bothered to take on small tasks at home this week. This is a good time to plan a change of décor. If you are invited out this weekend by a member of the opposite sex, be on your best behaviour and make a good impression.

Your lucky numbers this week: 1, 12, 15, 31.

6–12 MAY 2000

Do not expect special favours. Influential people will not be willing to grant an increase in salary, to promote you, or to allow you to knock off work earlier than usual. Disagreements will occur if you try to press your demands. Accept the situation in which you find yourself. Home will be the best place for you this week.

Your lucky numbers this week: 10, 15, 26, 29.

13–19 MAY 2000

Do all you can to bring happiness into the lives of loved ones. It will give you great pleasure to put a smile on the face of your partner or child. You will certainly reap great satisfaction from giving to others. Entertainment will be easy to find and is unlikely to put you to extraordinary expense.

Your lucky numbers this week: 1, 12, 19, 31.

20–26 MAY 2000

This rather restful week will come as a welcome break. Slow down; you let your nerves get rather wound up on occasion. Nothing will interfere with your regular tasks. Do not try to start anything new, as conditions will be far too quiet to branch out new ideas. Roosters who have been suffering from minor ailments should be able to get satisfactory treatment now.

Your lucky numbers this week: 2, 11, 19, 36.

27 MAY–2 JUNE 2000

If you think there is a plot against you at work, you are probably dreaming. Colleagues are willing to help you whenever you need them. Romantic involvements with older people will be sticky; perhaps the age gap is too great to be bridged.

Your lucky numbers this week: 9, 12, 15, 31.

3–9 JUNE 2000

All of your important work is likely to be achieved midweek. Differences with loved ones can be smoothed out; this bodes well for the whole week. People you meet will lack energy. Outdoor activities are unlikely to appeal. No important changes in the way finances are handled should be attempted.

Your lucky numbers this week: 1, 10, 18, 32.

10–16 JUNE 2000

Restraint is vital in all matters connected with money. Pay small bills, check your bank statement and try to discover exactly how you stand as far as savings are concerned. Do what you can to explain the situation to the more extravagant members of your family. This is not a time when any of your brood can afford to go on a spending spree.

Your lucky numbers this week: 9, 11, 19, 33.

17–23 JUNE 2000

This week will fly by. There will be a number of things to deal with in faraway places. Handle them in person, as this will be much more effective than trying to sort out issues over the phone or in letters. The personal touch is needed. Useful information that will enable you to advance your creative projects can be obtained.

Your lucky numbers this week: 10, 11, 19, 32.

24–30 JUNE 2000

People at a distance will continue to be extremely co-operative. You will find it easier to deal with newcomers than with your usual business contacts. The new and the untried will be a stimulus. Routine business will be rather difficult to concentrate on. This is not a good week for dealing with authority figures. Wait before discussing your future career prospects.

Your lucky numbers this week: 1, 12, 18, 33.

1 JULY–7 JULY 2000

There is an element of deception this week. Someone at your place of employment may be out to hoodwink you for some reason. Everything that you are told in connection with your business needs to be verified. Perhaps a colleague wants you to make a fool of yourself in the eyes of a superior. A certain amount of jealousy is at play.

Your lucky numbers this week: 1, 2, 24, 26.

8–14 JULY 2000

You are probably not thinking straight. This is the wrong week to follow hunches or to make snap decisions. Speculative propositions should be avoided and, gambling could be disastrous. Take special care when travelling this week.

Your lucky numbers this week: 11, 12, 15, 33.

15–21 JULY 2000

Probably the best week this month, if not this year. You will be extremely aware of everything going on around you. Your sense of intuition will be particularly strong. You will have the chance to display your merits to important people. It may be possible to leapfrog over competitors into a job that you have been keen to take on. Even romance is starred. Whether single or married, you will be happy in the company of that special person in your life.

Your lucky numbers this week: 11, 12, 19, 32.

22–28 JULY 2000

Conditions continue to favour Roosters. Creative projects are likely to progress. This is not a good week, however, for borrowing or lending money. Friends may ask you for a helping hand. If you do get involved with other people's problems, try to be businesslike about getting paid back. In this way you will safeguard your own interests and probably save your friendship from being disrupted or totally ruined.

Your lucky numbers this week: 2, 10, 15, 34.

29 JULY–4 AUGUST 2000

You are at your peak. You represent a commanding presence in the life of those around you, even if you do not know this is the case. When finally wake up to the fact, a period of great influence lies before you. Take advantage of the matter and move forward on all fronts at once.

Your lucky numbers this week: 1, 12, 19, 33.

5–11 AUGUST 2000

What happens at work this week will upset your calculations for the months ahead. You may have to lower your sights temporarily. Do not be disillusioned, however, as things will work out to your advantage. This weekend is a bad time for romance. Partners are likely to be difficult and argumentative.

Your lucky numbers this week: 9, 10, 25, 32.

12–18 AUGUST 2000

Things are bound to slow down a little at the beginning of the week, but this is only temporary. You tend to be short of energy and time, so try to find ways and means of using both rather carefully.

Your lucky numbers this week: 1, 21, 31, 33.

19–25 AUGUST 2000

You can put invitations to good use now. It does not matter whether proposals come in business or in your social life; you cannot turn them down. Although it is still some time away, you may well have your sights firmly fixed on the next summer period and your hopes for it.

Your lucky numbers this week: 5, 12, 24, 36.

26 AUGUST–1 SEPTEMBER 2000

With potentially exciting things going on in all areas of your life this week, there is nothing to prevent you from being cheerful and positive in your general approach. Not everyone is inclined to agree with you at present, though you do have the persuasive powers to bring almost anyone round to your point of view this week.

Your lucky numbers this week: 1, 13, 15, 31.

2–8 SEPTEMBER 2000

At work the week will not turn out as planned. Things will go awry right from the start. You may take matters in your stride, provided you are willing and adaptable enough to make one or two hasty changes.

Your lucky numbers this week: 2, 12, 15, 33.

9–15 SEPTEMBER 2000

Meet people halfway and follow compromise solutions wherever you can. You will not go far if you try to be independent. This is the right time to consider the future. Pay attention to matters concerning security in old age. Invest in your own future, rather than splurging on perishables.

Your lucky numbers this week: 1, 19, 25, 31.

16–22 SEPTEMBER 2000

An excellent period for all romantic matters. You are clearly able to let your partner know how you feel concerning just about anything, and you have more than enough cheek to carry out a bold personal plan. Whenever you need support, you should find that it is ready and waiting in the wings. This is a period for action.

Your lucky numbers this week: 3, 12, 15, 34.

23–29 SEPTEMBER 2000

Many single Roosters could be carried away more by the thought of romance than by the romance itself. Do not believe all that people tell you. You are likely to deceive yourself in matters of the heart. Married Roosters will not have this sort of problem, as partners are co-operative and a happy week is indicated.

Your lucky numbers this week: 1, 10, 15, 31.

30 SEPTEMBER–6 OCTOBER 2000

This is another busy week, but ensure that you know what is expected of you. Nobody can tell you how to behave, even if that is exactly how most individuals seem to be acting. A fresh approach to an old problem can help you out no end by the weekend.

Your lucky numbers this week: 2, 12, 19, 33.

7–13 OCTOBER 2000

Do not be at all reluctant to think big; there is every chance that you can make your most grandiose schemes pay off this week. People have powerful reactions, leading you to believe that you have it in you to get away with almost anything that occurs to you.

Your lucky numbers this week: 1, 10, 15, 31.

14–20 OCTOBER 2000

Financial problems lead you into consultation with your bank manager or superior. Begging letters will achieve nothing; simply outline your problem and you will get a sympathetic hearing – and possibly some help. This is a good week for romance, however; new partnerships could be long-lasting.

Your lucky numbers this week: 2, 12, 17, 33.

21–27 OCTOBER 2000

A week for romance. You will probably be travelling around on cloud nine because of a recent introduction, though this is unlikely to be a lasting affair; make the most of it while you can. Invitations for this weekend will be more than you can handle.

Your lucky numbers this week: 1, 12, 15, 36.

28 OCTOBER–3 NOVEMBER 2000

Do not be tempted out by friends. Problems will be found in their company. Better by far that you stay at home to catch up with domestic chores. DIY jobs will not go amiss and you will be able to lose yourself in whatever you turn your hand to.

Your lucky numbers this week: 2, 13, 15, 33.

4–10 NOVEMBER 2000

Younger members of the staff brighten up what threatens to be a dull day. Finances receive a boost, thanks to a shrewd investment paying dividends. In-laws could cause problems on the domestic front, if they are allowed to influence your partner. Children are a source of irritation this weekend.

Your lucky numbers this week: 11, 12, 25, 32.

11–17 NOVEMBER 2000

This is a socially eventful week. Invitations arrive like snow-flakes; be wise and only accept those where you know you will have fun. It is time to forget politics at work and get down to enjoying yourself. Those involved in the entertainment industry will receive bad news from a partner.

Your lucky numbers this week: 1, 12, 20, 32.

18–24 NOVEMBER 2000

On shopping sprees, react positively to any bargains offered this week. An extremely good purchase will be made. Unexpected news in the mail from someone living at a distance will set you thinking about moving house.

Your lucky numbers this week: 8, 10, 19, 34.

25 NOVEMBER–1 DECEMBER 2000

You have a clear road ahead this week, with little standing in your way. Some may even consider the week's activities to be rather boring, but thank your lucky stars you have no problems to contend with. Financial gains should be made this weekend. All in all, quite an enjoyable week in front of you!

Your lucky numbers this week: 1, 12, 15, 31.

2–8 DECEMBER 2000

A busy end to the working month, and a week that is both interesting and eventful. It might seem on occasion that too many people are expressing their viewpoints at the same time, which can make your head spin. However, this is an ideal time to reach a sensible agreement.

Your lucky numbers this week: 2, 22, 23, 35.

9–15 DECEMBER 2000

A good week for completing any outstanding tasks around the home. Courtesy calls should be made, especially if they involve travel – this is one of the few good weeks available for this activity. In no uncertain terms romance bites the dust this weekend, because of a broken promise.

Your lucky numbers this week: 4, 11, 21, 36.

16–22 DECEMBER 2000

Much going on behind the scenes should interest you and stimulate your imagination. A social event will turn out to be just as you expected and you will do yourself a lot of good by showing your face. Parents are warned that children are likely to be irritating and demanding.

Your lucky numbers this week: 1, 12, 25, 32.

23–29 DECEMBER 2000

Visiting people who can back your artistic ideas is likely to be an utter waste of time. Set your feet firmly back on the ground. This is a week for using logic rather following hunches. Agreements have to be negotiated with much caution.

Your lucky numbers this week: 10, 13, 19, 33.

30 DECEMBER–5 JANUARY 2001

If travelling this week you should leave instructions about where to be reached in case of emergency. Minor health problems within the family may develop into something more ominous if proper precautions are not taken. You could benefit financially from the mistake of a work colleague.

Your lucky numbers this week: 1, 12, 15, 31.

6–12 JANUARY 2001

Differences with influential people may be avoidable. You will find it extremely hard to work under pressure, and your boss's ideas about how a job should be done is apt to clash with the way you feel about it. A good week for you who can focus most of their attention at home.

Your lucky numbers this week: 3, 12, 17, 28.

13–19 JANUARY 2001

Freedom from pressure lets you do as you please. Personal relationships will be much on your mind. You will be keen to iron out differences with loved ones. This can be done with calm, frank discussions, where nobody loses their temper. Friends will be agreeable. You will probably be in the mood for mixed company.

Your lucky numbers this week: 10, 22, 25, 30.

20–26 JANUARY 2001 (24 JANUARY: CHINESE NEW YEAR – YEAR OF THE SNAKE)

Boldly confront what must be done. Do not try to wriggle out of your responsibilities, and throw yourself into your job. There is no way to solve your financial problems through gambling. Once you grasp what is bothering you, coping with it will not be that difficult.

Your lucky numbers this week: 11, 12, 15, 32.

THE SIGN OF THE
Dog

The Chinese name for the Dog: Gou
The eleventh sign in the Chinese zodiac
The hours governed by the Dog: 7pm–9pm
The corresponding sign in the Western zodiac: Aries
Element: Metal
The direction of the pole: Positive

*

The Year of the Dog in the Western Calendar

10 February 1910–29 January 1911 Metal Dog
28 January 1922–15 February 1923 Water Dog
14 February 1934–3 February 1935 Wood Dog
2 February 1946–21 January 1947 Fire Dog
18 February 1958–7 February 1959 Earth Dog
6 February 1970–26 January 1971 Metal Dog
25 January 1982–12 February 1983 Water Dog
10 February 1994–30 January 1995 Wood Dog
29 January 2006–17 February 2007 Fire Dog

Famous People Born Under the Sign of the Dog

André Agassi, Brigitte Bardot, Candice Bergen, David Bowie, Kate Bush, Naomi Campbell, King Carl XVI Gustav of Sweden, Cher, Sir Winston Churchill, Petula Clark, Bill Clinton, Henry Cooper, Jamie Lee Curtis, John Dunn, Sally Field, Zsa Zsa Gabor, Ava Gardner, Michael Jackson, Sophia Loren, Shirley MacLaine, Madonna, Norman Mailer, Winnie Mandela, Golda Meir, Liza Minnelli, David Niven, Sydney Pollack, Elvis Presley, Prince, Sade, Alan Shearer, Claudia Schiffer, Norman Schwarzkopf, Albert Schweizer, Sylvester Stallone, Sharon Stone, Mother Teresa, Voltaire, Prince William, Shelley Winters.

The Dog in a Nutshell

POSITIVE QUALITIES
Faithful, generous, honest and observant.

NEGATIVE QUALITIES
Worried, pessimistic and a little absent-minded.

CAREER SUGGESTIONS
Customs officer, policeman, instructor, actor or reporter.

Main Features of the Dog

You are solid and faithful, but tend to be overly careful and pessimistic. It is wise not to worry too much beforehand, because you will get along whatever happens.

LUCK
Either you are very rich, or you do not own a pin. The different types of Dogs have different fates in store, but most of you are positive and go through life with great faith in succeeding.

MONEY
You have talents with money, and you are good at following up on business. If you follow your intuition, then you may have the chance to go far.

WORK

You are a loyal employee and you will reach the top, because you are also a good administrator. Before long you will be the boss.

SOCIAL LIFE

You can be very reserved and careful, but you thrive on being in the company of people you know well.

BUSINESS

You are skilful in managing your projects and keeping things on schedule, but you may have put up a bit of a fight for yourself. Place your feet firmly on the ground and do not give up without a fight.

LOVE

It will take you a long time to find your loved one, as you are very demanding and particular. But once you find the right person, you will enjoy a caring and romantic relationship.

PARENTS

Your parents are either very fond of you, or they will regard you as a rebel who is constantly fighting. It is of course up to you to tackle such a situation.

SISTERS AND BROTHERS

You take good care of your sisters and brothers, especially if you are the oldest one in the family, in which case you will have great influence on their grown-up lives.

CHILDREN

As parents you are tough and strict, but in truth you are deeply involved with your children and love them to the utmost.

TRAVEL

Travelling is something you really get excited about. You are always looking for the best possible place to spend a wonderful holiday with your close ones.

HEALTH

You are strong and you seldom fall ill. At times you get very tense, and you might have some mental problems if you are not careful.

INVESTMENTS

You will be making good money in property and brokerage because you just have a strong sense of money.

TALENTS

You are faithful and generous. You would make a good administrator for a large corporation. You are adept at net-working and you certainly know how to create profits.

PROSPECTS

If you stop grumbling and find faith in your abilities, then you will go far.

What Kind of Dog Are You?

THE WOOD DOG 1934, 1994

This is a fine watchdog. You are good at telling the truth, are always active and want to put things right. You will be famous and reach your planned goals.

THE FIRE DOG 1946, 2006

You are a pet; you do not need to toil or strive too much. Within a reasonable time you will become famous and powerful. Your life will be easy and full of opportunities.

EARTH DOG 1958, 2018

This is the mountain Dog, who thrives in the woods and the forests. You are clever and independent. Though there will be some problems in your younger years, you will have a nice and happy old age. You can make your name in the arts.

METAL DOG 1910, 1970

This is the Dog who lives in the temple. You thrive on being with people who are learned and wise. Your life will be happy and you will especially have an enjoyable old age.

WATER DOG 1922, 1982

You are a family Dog, and like to help people in your surroundings. You will have many hectic days, but enjoy being helpful to others. You are fond of travelling, and can be quite adventurous. You will have a good and interesting life.

The Ascendants of the Dog

11PM–1AM: THE HOUR OF THE RAT 'ZI'
The Dog in you wants to be righteous and impartial, but the Rat in you does not care if you acquire your money at the expense of the Dog's conscience. Luckily, this is also a very strong combination for you to become a famous writer or journalist.

1AM–3AM: THE HOUR OF THE OX 'ZHOU'
A serious fighter for justice who could be rather boring if you are not saved by the Dog's stable temper. You are at least willing to listen to what others have to say before you judge them.

3AM–5AM: THE HOUR OF THE TIGER 'YIN'
You are a very reasonable and co-operative person, which results from the Dog in you. The bad temper of the Tiger is moderated by the Dog's willingness to compromise, but your mouth is as sharp as a razor.

5AM–7AM: THE HOUR OF THE RABBIT 'MAO'
The Dog becomes more open and friendly because of the influence of the Rabbit. You will be less self-occupied and care for others less fortunate than yourself. You are a very honest and comfortable Dog with many admirers.

7AM–9AM: THE HOUR OF THE DRAGON 'ZHEN'
You are the one who inspires confidence and, with reason, one can give you friendship and rely on your word. With this combination you are a loyal and dedicated creature who appreciates the luck that comes your way throughout life.

9AM–11AM: THE HOUR OF THE SNAKE 'SI'
With the Snake you have a keen moral sense and are intuitive, but have a tendency to be rather pessimistic. Life with you can become very complicated. You are the kind to torment yourself to excess, expecting a hurricane with the slightest gust of wind, or a deluge after a few drops of rain. You are always on the watch and constantly on guard. Do try to relax.

11AM–1PM: THE HOUR OF THE HORSE 'WU'

You are loyal and tenaciously make your way by day and night, prodded by your intuition. You succeed in controlling both your pride and your fear of failure, never hesitating to smile at your own defects and weaknesses, yet remaining ardent and passionate. You are truly reliable.

1PM–3PM: THE HOUR OF THE GOAT 'WEI'

You are gifted with remarkable intuition. Unfortunately you often complicate your life, forever changing your moods, ideas and decisions, constantly retracing your steps and becoming distrustful and pessimistic. You will be faithful and courageous.

3PM–5PM: THE HOUR OF THE MONKEY 'SHEN'

You are extremely intuitive, and it will be difficult to put you off your trail; you will always find your way despite obstacles and difficulties. However, you have a tendency to make things complicated because, to you, everything is just a game and it all depends on how long you want to take part. You hate simplicity, straight lines and mapped-out routes.

5PM–7PM: THE HOUR OF THE ROOSTER 'YU'

This talkative Dog can never be quiet. You would rather talk than go into action. You are clever, with good judgement, and it is easy for you to get what you want. The problem is that often you talk so much that valuable time is lost. Anyway, you will persevere, though without any desire for conquest or revenge.

7PM–9PM: THE HOUR OF THE DOG 'XU'

This defensive Dog is forever on guard. You are always looking for something that you can fight for or against. You are frank and righteous, but you are also a rebel. You will be a fighter and a revolutionary, but not least a pessimist.

9PM–11PM: THE HOUR OF THE PIG 'HAI'

This is a nice, modest Dog who does not hesitate to take the paths away from the main roads. By doing so, you will gain self-confidence. Your natural self-doubt will be less apparent and weigh less on your companions. You will always remain an enigmatic and mysterious person to those around you.

The Year Ahead

The Dog has always been considered pessimistic and anxious, though the origin of his torments is rarely investigated, but the Dog is the faithful companion of man, an affectionate pet and even important as a status symbol. The life of the Dog, as told by the ancient Chinese, will often be unstable, except during childhood (though only if his parents are protective enough). His youth is often tormented with difficult love affairs, which rarely leave him with pleasant memories. His maturity will be haunted by nightmares, and his old age saddened by regrets at failing to have made the most of life when he had the chance. But luckily there are different kinds of Dog – life is easier for some, and more exciting and difficult for others. It is said that Dogs that are born during daytime are luckier than those during the night. The Dog of the day will not have to be on guard, while the Dog of the night will have to be on watch all the time.

Women Dogs are more ambitious and aspire more to material security. You are gifted and creative, but you are slightly lacking in perseverance and may leave things half-finished. You are also attractive, impatient and adore deep conversation, being more sociable than your counterpart Mr Dog. You are happiest when surrounded by friends, children and pets – be it in a palace, a suburban house or a city flat. Your only fault lies in a tendency towards narrow-mindedness, an inability to appreciate things which are not part of your immediate universe.

A very favourable year with many inspiring tasks if you know how to make use of the year. In money matters you continue the successes of last year. You are striving to reach the top, and you want to have full control over the situation. In the last part you will tend to be more philosophical and examine your present life with different eyes. You will have many interesting opportunities in this period. Sweet music will arise between you and your partner, and he or she will think of you in a different way. This year will be outstanding if you learn how to apply and make use of your possibilities.

Week By Week For People Born Under the Sign of the Dog

5–11 FEBRUARY 2000 (5 FEBRUARY: CHINESE NEW YEAR – YEAR OF THE DRAGON)

There will be ideal opportunities to bloom in your place of employment again, if you only learn how to make things go in your favour. The best way to catch the eye of your boss is to show you are hard-working and can knuckle down to a job. You can do much to dispel any doubts about your reliability. Prove that you can grit your teeth and keep up to schedule.

Your lucky numbers this week: 11, 12, 15, 32.

12–18 FEBRUARY 2000

An erratic week. You will be more dependent on others than usual. There are likely to be delays because of late arrivals at the office or factory. No matter how much you are irritated by your colleagues, try not to lose your temper. Associates will be impulsive. Do not rely on verbal promises.

Your lucky numbers this week: 12, 19, 33, 34.

19–25 FEBRUARY 2000

A pleasant week for you and your family. Problems that have been in the back of your mind will be easier to deal with. Have a frank chat with your beloved, and explain what has been worrying you. It would be best to bring differences out into the open and clear the air. Chances are that you will be drawn closer to your partner than you have been for some time. Creative work will become important this week.

Your lucky numbers this week: 2, 10, 15, 34.

26 FEBRUARY–3 MARCH 2000

Some uncertainty will make this week rather difficult. You will not be able to agree with your partner or parent on how to spend your spare time. Your ideas are unlikely to be acceptable to members of your family. Once you reach a compromise, it should be possible to enjoy activities.

Your lucky numbers this week: 10, 12, 25, 32.

4–10 MARCH 2000

This week will be marked by a lack of activity. Nothing of any significance will occur, nor should you try to make anything happen. Deal with any backlog of work that has mounted up. There are minor chores that you have been avoiding; this week affords the perfect chance for you to put your affairs in order.

Your lucky numbers this week: 1, 12, 15, 35.

11–17 MARCH 2000

Nothing is likely to run according to plan. It would be best not to make too many important appointments. People will not be very reliable. Before setting off on a journey, check to be sure the people you want to see have not forgotten the engagement. If you are careful, things will work out right for you.

Your lucky numbers this week: 11, 17, 19, 32.

18–24 MARCH 2000

Continue to be extremely careful about your financial situation this week. Leave nothing to chance as far as cash is concerned. Investments made now are unlikely to bring in anticipated returns; this is not a time to look for easy ways of making money.

Your lucky numbers this week: 11, 22, 25, 33.

25–31 MARCH 2000

Stick to familiar surroundings. You will not achieve much if you try to drum up support for your ideas in other places. Dogs who earn their living through buying and selling may find their earnings dipping considerably, especially if most of their income comes from commissions. Relatives will be difficult. Try to keep out of non-productive arguments.

Your lucky numbers this week: 4, 12, 15, 32.

1 APRIL–7 APRIL 2000

Confrontations with influential people may be avoidable. You will find it extremely difficult to work under pressure. Your boss's ideas about how a job should be done are apt to differ from your own opinion. This is a good week for Dogs who can concentrate their energies on the home.

Your lucky numbers this week: 1, 12, 19, 34.

8–14 APRIL 2000

Business results could be interesting this week. What you must bear in mind is that greater self-reliance is essential to significant progress. This is not a week when you can afford to sit back and wait for the phone to ring.

Your lucky numbers this week: 4, 12, 15, 36.

15–21 APRIL 2000

You should make every effort to bring yourself to the attention of superiors early this week, as little progress will be made later on. If attending discussions or business meetings, be sure that you are noticed. Domestic upheavals will upset partners but stimulate you.

Your lucky numbers this week: 1, 18, 19, 30.

22–28 APRIL 2000

Probably a slightly better week for dealing with superiors. It will be easier to handle routine work, and you will have little difficulty with concentration. Teamwork should produce useful results. Co-operating with your colleagues will help stave off boredom. Dogs in business partnerships have to be extra careful this week.

Your lucky numbers this week: 1, 11, 15, 32.

29 APRIL–5 MAY 2000

Catch up with odd jobs this week in order to make life easier in the weeks to come. This will be a fairly quiet time. No pressure is likely within the home or outside it. People you come into contact with will be congenial but disinclined to get involved in anything too energetic.

Your lucky numbers this week: 3, 10, 19, 33.

6–12 MAY 2000

Emotionally this could be one of the most upsetting weeks that Dogs have had to face for some time. Those of you who are unmarried will be worrying about the way a relationship is developing. Parents will be particularly concerned for their children's welfare.

Your lucky numbers this week: 1, 12, 15, 32.

13–19 MAY 2000

You should be prepared to take a few chances. You will be in tune with a work colleague and joint ventures will be successful. Domestic partnerships could suffer from a lack of attention on your part. Romantic matters are also going through a sticky period.

Your lucky numbers this week: 9, 11, 29, 34.

20–26 MAY 2000

Work will be pleasant this week. The atmosphere at your workplace will be conducive to good results. Colleagues are willing to follow any lead that you give, so new ideas you have been waiting to implement can now be attempted with success.

Your lucky numbers this week: 1, 22, 25, 32.

27 May–2 June 2000

Try to improve labour relations. Dog bosses who have to deal with trade unions should do all that they can to improve their understanding of the problems of their work force. It will be easier to have your ideas accepted if you show personal interest in your employees. This week favours romantic pursuits.

Your lucky numbers this week: 11, 12, 15, 35.

3–9 June 2000

Differences in opinion with your partner will easily develop, perhaps because of something that happened over the course of last week. Plans suggested to you are unlikely to be acceptable. You will be quite pleased to get out of the domestic environment this week.

Your lucky numbers this week: 3, 10, 19, 30.

10–16 June 2000

Use your brain rather than brawn this week. Additional money can be made through increased mental activity rather than physical energy. Creative enterprises can be made more valuable by joining forces with people who have specialized knowledge that you appear to lack. There will be no need to go it alone. This is an excellent week for teamwork on any level.

Your lucky numbers this week: 1, 12, 15, 32.

17–23 June 2000

Travel should be postponed this week as this is not a good period for making long journeys, whether for business or for pleasure. If you cannot avoid it, then be particularly cautious of driving. Take no risks on the road. Check your car before setting out, especially tyre pressure.

Your lucky numbers this week: 6, 12, 19, 30.

24–30 June 2000

An extremely happy week for activities around the home. There will be good opportunities to improve your relationship with your partner. Unspoken differences can now be discussed to everybody's benefit. An engagement this week is likely to lead to a happy marriage.

Your lucky numbers this week: 1, 12, 18, 33.

1 JULY–7 JULY 2000

You will find it difficult to understand the impulsive actions of loved ones. Plans you were keen to carry out in connection with your home may not be acceptable to them. It is also possible that someone is trying to pull the wool over your eyes. Deception lurks in the air. Matters at work will be relatively simple compared with the domestic situation. This is a good week for experimenting with new working methods.

Your lucky numbers this week: 11, 12, 15, 24.

8–14 JULY 2000

It is quite likely that the problems of loved ones will interfere with your own plans. A member of your family may not be feeling too well, so it might be necessary to cancel reservations. Do not be too disappointed if entertainment you have been looking forward to for some time has to be postponed at the last minute at the weekend.

Your lucky numbers this week: 1, 19, 25, 32.

15–21 JULY 2000

If you can control your impulsive tendencies, this will be a good week for business. Beware of your extravagant streak. If you play your cards right, you could increase your earnings considerably in the not too distant future. A more romantic week than usual will be awaiting you.

Your lucky numbers this week: 2, 10, 19, 33.

22–28 JULY 2000

No one and nothing can disturb your plans for this week. This will be a highly enjoyable week, when you can do exactly as you please. Pressures at home and work should be reduced considerably. Trips and visits will be successful, especially if you are visiting close friends or relatives you have not seen for some time. They will be pleased to see you.

Your lucky numbers this week: 2, 3, 25, 31.

29 JULY–4 AUGUST 2000

You will have to find compromises wherever you can. You will not get far if you try to do things alone. This is the right time to think about the future. Pay attention to matters regarding security in old age. Invest in your own future rather than splashing out on things of short-lived value.

Your lucky numbers this week: 11, 12, 15, 32.

5–11 AUGUST 2000

An excellent period for all romantic interests. You are clearly able to let your partner know how you feel concerning just about any aspect of life, and you have more than enough cheek to carry out a daring personal plan. When you need support, you should find that it is ready and waiting in the wings. This is a period for action.

Your lucky numbers this week: 1, 12, 19, 22.

12–18 AUGUST 2000

This is a very busy week, but make certain that you know what is expected of you. Nobody can really tell you how you should behave, though that may seem exactly what is happening right now. A new approach to an old problem can help you out no end by the weekend.

Your lucky numbers this week: 7, 11, 17, 35.

19–25 AUGUST 2000

Do not be reluctant about thinking big, because there is every chance that you can make your most grandiose schemes pay off this week. Reactions are extraordinary and lead you to believe that you have the potential to achieve almost anything that occurs to you.

Your lucky numbers this week: 1, 12, 15, 32.

26 AUGUST–1 SEPTEMBER 2000

Things are still looking good, though probably becoming quieter as the weekend approaches. Now you should turn your attention towards your personal life, which looks more exciting than it has done for ages. Clear any obstacles from your path quickly.

Your lucky numbers this week: 9, 16, 22, 23.

2–8 SEPTEMBER 2000

Deep thinking provides new personal insights into all sorts of personal matters. This does not prevent you from being yourself or from doing what comes naturally in a business and social sense. You might fancy a change of scene after work and can probably spend some time with a person who is special.

Your lucky numbers this week: 1, 12, 15, 32.

9–15 SEPTEMBER 2000

Family and domestic matters now take up most of your time, leaving you little energy to create the space to develop your career. Patience is required, but you might find this hard to summon up at the moment. Experience and common sense count in most situations right now.

Your lucky numbers this week: 3, 12, 15, 33.

16–22 SEPTEMBER 2000

The domestic sphere of life continues to take up much of your time, and you may be planning to spend more time with your close ones this week. Meanwhile you need to finish the more practical aspects in this period, so that you can continue with them in a more positive way next week.

Your lucky numbers this week: 10, 12, 15, 33.

23–29 SEPTEMBER 2000

You should now be able to spend upon practical matters and even turn rather difficult situations to your own advantage. It is only a matter of time before you discover that a problem is about to be solved. You will be happy to put on your thinking cap for the benefit of a friend.

Your lucky numbers this week: 7, 8, 21, 30.

30 SEPTEMBER–6 OCTOBER 2000

You want to have fun. Pleasure and travel will be important this week, so there will probably not be enough time to deal with practical matters that this period might demand. Keep an eye on finances, which are probably not very strong at the moment. It will not be long before they improve, at the end of the week.

Your lucky numbers this week: 5, 6, 8, 30.

7–13 OCTOBER 2000

Very good news is on the way, probably from a good friend abroad. The positive side of this is that you can use what is said as a platform for your own ideas. Creating more space for yourself is also important in what should be a positive week.

Your lucky numbers this week: 2, 16, 27, 30.

14–20 OCTOBER 2000

Things are bound to slow down a little bit at the beginning of the week, but this is only short-lived. You tend to lack both energy and time, so make sure you use both rather carefully. Otherwise this will be a quiet and peaceful week.

Your lucky numbers this week: 10, 12, 15, 32.

21–27 OCTOBER 2000

This week is good for contacting your friends. An invitation will not be far off as they are eager to see you. Your social life is experiencing an up-turn. Although the weather may be on the turn, you are already planning ahead to next summer. However, you might not have the patience to wait and a long trip to somewhere warm could be in sight.

Your lucky numbers this week: 9, 10, 15, 33.

28 OCTOBER–3 NOVEMBER 2000

With potentially exciting things happening in all areas of life this week, there is nothing to stop you from being cheerful and positive in your general approach. Not everyone is on the same wavelength as you at present, but you do have the persuasive powers to bring almost anyone round to your point of view this week.

Your lucky numbers this week: 1, 12, 19, 32.

4–10 NOVEMBER 2000

Professional and career projects bring certain pressures to bear that you could happily do without. Remaining calm and relaxed under most circumstances however, you are likely to allow the slight irritations of the week to alter your perspective. Not everyone around you turns out to be equally helpful.

Your lucky numbers this week: 6, 8, 29, 30.

11–17 NOVEMBER 2000

You need a greater capacity for self-expression. Metaphorically speaking, it is a time of both sunshine and showers. Even when slight difficulties arise, you can deal with them easily.

Your lucky numbers this week: 8, 12, 15, 22.

18–24 NOVEMBER 2000

An excellent time for getting away from things. This probably means that for once you become something of a hermit, which will certainly not suit everyone you come encounter at present. A slow and steady pace leads you to an exciting event just around the corner.

Your lucky numbers this week: 1, 18, 19, 32.

25 NOVEMBER–1 DECEMBER 2000

Co-operation is the keynote. This is a splendid period for reaching agreement with your partner on the best way to handle mutual affairs. It is also a good time to start work on your home, for example with painting or redecorating. Anything that gives you an opportunity to be artistic will appeal to you. Speculation could bring luck for a change. This is a week for travel and dealing with long-distance affairs.

Your lucky numbers this week: 2, 11, 12, 36.

2–8 DECEMBER 2000

If you can control impulsive tendencies, this will be a good week for business. Watch your extravagant streak. You may suddenly feel like spending. Things you are tempted to buy will be luxury items of little practical use. Worthwhile agreements can be consummated with people in superior positions and if you play your cards right, you could increase your income considerably in the not too distant future. People will be generally helpful and sympathetic to your aims.

Your lucky numbers this week: 10, 12, 15, 34.

9–15 DECEMBER 2000

Work will tend to be strenuous. You will have some difficulty following your schedule this week, nor will it be easy to promote teamwork. You must rely on yourself more than usual. You are good with words, but the gift of the gab may desert you. Your health continues to require attention. A week where you should tread cautiously.

Your lucky numbers this week: 1, 3, 12, 30.

16–22 DECEMBER 2000

Nobody and nothing is likely to interfere with the Dog's plans for this week. This will be one of those enjoyable times when you can do exactly as you please. Home and job pressures ought to be reduced considerably. Get out and about more. If you feel you have been getting in a rut, do something for a change. Trips and visits will be successful, especially if you are visiting friends or relatives you have not see for some time.

Your lucky numbers this week: 9, 12, 15, 32.

23–29 DECEMBER 2000

You will have to keep a check on your tongue and the business prospects this week will be great. If you stop pouring money out of your pockets and play your cards right you could soon win the rewards you are after. This is a more giving and romantic week than usual.

Your lucky numbers this week: 1, 12, 15, 22.

30 DECEMBER–5 JANUARY 2001

You are your own boss this week, and no one will interfere with your plans. This could be an unforgettable week in which you do exactly as you please. All you choose to do at home and work will be problem-free. Travel will be successful, especially if you are visiting dear friends or relatives you have not seen for some time. They will love seeing you again.

Your lucky numbers this week: 9, 12, 15, 32.

6–12 JANUARY 2001

Fun and pleasure are paramount now, You move forward because you can make practical things happen as you go. No matter how you feel about a new project you should at least give others the benefit of the doubt. You need to stay away from negative thinking in all forms.

Your lucky numbers this week: 1, 12, 15, 36.

13–19 JANUARY 2001

This is another very constructive week, but make certain that you know what is expected of you in advance. Nobody can really tell you how to behave at the moment, even if that seems to be the case. New perspectives on old problems will be important by the weekend.

Your lucky numbers this week: 2, 3, 6, 30.

20–26 JANUARY 2001 (24 JANUARY: CHINESE NEW YEAR – YEAR OF THE SNAKE)

At work you must get on with whatever seems important. Although you probably do not really care for certain tasks, these are intermixed with more interesting matters that can catch your imagination. You may have to be brave at some stage.

Your lucky numbers this week: 1, 14, 18, 33.

THE SIGN OF THE
Pig

The Chinese name for the Pig: Zhu
The twelfth sign in the Chinese zodiac
The hours governed by the Pig: 9pm–11pm
The corresponding sign in the Western zodiac: Pisces
Element: Metal
The direction of the pole: Negative

*

The Year of the Pig in the Western Calendar

30 January 1911–17 February 1912 Metal Pig
16 February 1923–4 February 1924 Water Pig
4 February 1935–23 January 1936 Wood Pig
22 January 1947–9 February 1948 Fire Pig
8 February 1959–27 January 1960 Earth Pig
27 January 1971–15 January 1972 Metal Pig
13 February 1983–1 February 1984 Water Pig
31 January 1995–18 February 1996 Wood Pig
18 February 2007–6 February 2008 Fire Pig

Famous People Born Under the Sign of the Pig

Bryan Adams, Woody Allen, Julie Andrews, Fred Astaire, Richard Attenborough, Hector Berlioz, Lucille Ball, Humphrey Bogart, James Cagney, Chiang Kai-shek, Hillary Clinton, Glenn Close, Oliver Cromwell, Robert Dole, Richard Dreyfuss, Farrah Fawcett, Henry Ford, Ernest Hemingway, Henry VIII, Barry Gibb, Alfred Hitchcock, Elton John, C.J. Jung, Henry Kissinger, Kevin Kline, Jerry Lee Lewis, John McEnroe, Viscount Montgomery of Alamein, Dudley Moore, John Mortimer, Wolfgang Amadeus Mozart, Marie Osmond, Michael Parkinson, Shimon Peres, Prince Rainier of Monaco, Maurice Ravel, Ronald Reagan, Lee Remick, Ginger Rogers, Albert Schweitzer, Arnold Schwarzenegger, Steven Spielberg, Emma Thompson, the Duchess of York.

The Pig in a Nutshell

POSITIVE QUALITIES
Generous, tolerant, gallant, honest, humorous, joyful, caring and intelligent.

NEGATIVE QUALITIES
Naïve, egotistic, moody, stubborn and likes flattery.

CAREER SUGGESTIONS
Actor, farmer, artist, as well as work where you feel you can give service to others.

Main Features of the Pig

You are kind and caring, but tend to be persistent and intense. However, you are enterprising, so that you are not as lazy as people might think you are.

LUCK
You are born under the sign of luck and fortune, the most favoured sign in the Chinese zodiac. You lack faith in yourself; if you can finally summon it, then fortune will follow you through life.

MONEY

You can become very rich by being pleasant to people around you.

WORK

You like people and are very service-minded. Work connected with people is something you want to get involved in. You are faithful and a good employee.

SOCIAL LIFE

You like parties or any kind of gatherings. You are a happy and joyful person who wants to take part in many different activities.

BUSINESS

Business is something you have a strong grip on. You will be praised for your efforts. Furthermore, you are good at following up on things and making them happen.

LOVE

You are very romantic and fond of the opposite sex. Since you are born under a lucky sign, you will have a healthy chance of meeting the love of your life and really falling in love.

PARENTS

You have parents who care about you. Your childhood passes without problems and is harmonious.

SISTERS AND BROTHERS

You can have a good relationship with siblings, as long as you do not make demands that are difficult for them to accept.

CHILDREN

You are fond of sex, so you will have many children. Luckily you understand that your children need much care and love, and are willing to sacrifice for them if necessary.

TRAVEL

You just love to travel and long to see what is beyond the mountains. Trips will bring you to far-off places you have been dreaming of.

HEALTH

You are strong, but you will probably have problems with your weight if you are careless. Pigs are fond of food and cannot keep away from delicious meals.

INVESTMENTS

No matter what you do, you will make money, simply because you are lucky.

TALENTS

You are generous and enterprising. Your luck and charm can take you far in life. Any work which involves dealing with people or looking after them can make your fortune.

PROSPECTS

You can expect a good life of joy and satisfaction, but you had better not be greedy or get yourself into heavy drinking. If you do, you will be in great trouble.

What Kind of Pig Are You?

THE WOOD PIG 1935, 1995

This is the Pig who likes action. You are kind and congenial to be with, but you can be a little bit too hasty with your words and deeds, so it is important to slow down and take one step at a time. You will have a good life and enjoy what results from your own success.

THE FIRE PIG 1947, 2007

This is the Pig that comes from the hills, a Pig that is wise and intelligent. You prefer to stand on your own feet, and are a little bit stubborn. If you can show more consideration to people around you, you will have a chance of reaching the top.

THE EARTH PIG 1959, 2019

This is the Pig who spends his time at the temple. You are clever and enterprising, and a little bit more spiritual than most. Your life floats leisurely forward, and you are always prepared to help people who are weaker than you are.

THE METAL PIG 1911, 1971

This is the Pig who stays at the farm. You prefer peace and calmness, and you can find a partner that you thrive with. Life is just wonderful and happy for you. Be careful, however, not to be exploited.

WATER PIG 1923, 1983

This is the mountain Pig. You are active and stubborn, but at the same time wise and clever. If you can teach yourself to be slightly more ambitious you can expect to be both rich and successful.

The Ascendants of the Pig

11PM–1AM: THE HOUR OF THE RAT 'ZI'

You are deadly charming and at times very selfish. You are also very fond of family life and take good care of the people around you. You are very curious, and could be a very good writer.

1AM–3AM: THE HOUR OF THE OX 'ZHOU'

A cosy Pig, though you might be very demanding and conservative. You lack the self-confidence to get things thoroughly done. Luckily you are very diligent, which serves as some sort of compensation. You are overly fond of food and forget to keep yourself in shape.

3AM–5AM: THE HOUR OF THE TIGER 'YIN'

You are a very impulsive and naïve Pig, happy and satisfied – as long as you get what you want. Though many people find you tiresome or possessive, this is because of your desire to find attention and friendship.

5AM–7AM: THE HOUR OF THE RABBIT 'MAO'

A solitary animal who is slightly unsettling and perfectly organized. You act rather mysteriously; one never knows what you are really up to. You are friendly, though, and when it is needed, you can even be very helpful.

7AM–9AM: THE HOUR OF THE DRAGON 'ZHEN'

With the Pig beside the Dragon, you are a solitary wanderer, seeking a treasure that perhaps you did not know how to protect. You tend to acquire material and spiritual wealth, and your life will never be dull.

9AM–11AM: THE HOUR OF THE SNAKE 'SI'

A quiet and philosophical Pig, you know what you want but you are also a bad loser. You prefer solitude to the risk of failure. You tend to have difficulties in making decisions. Sometimes the Pig in you will trick the Snake, leading you into trouble.

11am–1pm: the Hour of the Horse 'Wu'

Blessed with clear intelligence, this combination is well aware of the pride that eats away at you. You have a tendency to overrate the true value of your possessions and conquests and to overlook their impermanence. Your ardour and impulsiveness often give way to doubt and mystery, but in the end you will succeed.

1pm–3pm: the Hour of the Goat 'Wei'

You are a very sentimental, self-sacrificing Pig, almost too nice and naïve. You work hard and handle your close ones with care. However, you can also be very stubborn and proud. You are slow to recognize your errors, though that does not prevent you from being tolerant and ready to forgive.

3pm–5pm: the Hour of the Monkey 'Shen'

You like to live in solitude. You see things very clearly and have a built-in lie detector that may even seem psychic. With the combination you are difficult to live with. You have your own ideas about life and will not tolerate having those of other people imposed on you.

5pm–7pm: the Hour of the Rooster 'Yu'

To others you seem a strange and solitary traveller. You stand out from the crowd with your attitude to life, rather than with your appearance. You will seek a hiding place where you can bury your treasure far from the eyes of the world.

7pm–9pm: the Hour of the Dog 'Xu'

A nice and modest Pig, you do not hesitate to take shady tracks off the beaten track. By doing so, you will gain self-confidence in your own way and your natural self-doubt will be less apparent and weigh less on your companions. You will always remain an enigmatic and mysterious person to those around you.

9pm–11pm: the Hour of the Pig 'Hai'

With two Pigs in you, you tend to be a solitary and unsociable animal who likes to get off the beaten track. You are an original, who dislikes casual company. You love to travel on unknown paths, seeking out the mysteries of life, taking shelter in thickets and shrubs while waiting for night to fall before continuing on your way. You are instinctive and intuitive, obeying only your own law.

The Year Ahead

In the Chinese horoscope, the Pig symbolizes courage, prosperity and nobility. The childhood of the Pig will be calm, peaceful and protected, youth will be burdened with many emotional difficulties and maturity with family problems. Pigs should make an effort to attain emotional stability. They will enjoy prosperous old age.

The sign of the Pig is the most honest and scrupulous of all the animals in the Chinese zodiac. As the Pig you come into the world with a trunk full of slightly old-fashioned sentiments such as goodness, altruism, indulgence and tolerance, seasoned with optimism and an admirable belief in the perfectability of mankind. But at times you will be misunderstood. Needless to say, the vultures immediately pounce and make mincemeat of you. Because of this, people tend to believe that you are naïve, credulous, overconfident, easy pickings and vaguely stupid.

Distinction will be necessary. As the Pig you are rather easily taken in, but only in the sense that you prefer to see the bright side. You try to put yourself in the place of others, and to understand the worst depravities. You believe that there always exists, somewhere, a pure flame of goodness, however tiny. It must be protected and maintained.

The woman Pig is faithful by nature, but demanding and highly discriminating. They can also be rather jealous and possessive, expecting partners to be equally honest and devoted in their feelings. This is one reason why you are very careful when choosing a mate. When you are satisfied and happy with a relationship, you are extremely reliable, peaceful and optimistic.

The Pig is lucky with money. When you are not earning it yourself, you will find that someone will give it to you, and you invariably end up rather wealthy. If you prefer to handle your business alone, then you are also quite a money machine. Cash will flow with very little effort on your part. You will never be short of money.

You have a comfortable year ahead. You will suddenly become more attentive to your own economic situation, though you are somewhat unrealistic about your relationship with your partner. You act more sensitively and demand more of your relationship, making changes in your life and developing new perspectives. If you are willing to sacrifice some of yourself, then this period will be very rewarding. Fortunately, the last part of the year will be more comfortable, when your partner gives you more attention and understanding.

Week By Week for People Born Under the Sign of the Pig

5–11 FEBRUARY 2000 (5 FEBRUARY: CHINESE NEW YEAR – YEAR OF THE DRAGON)

The Chinese New Year starts rather favourably. You should now have the time to devote to practical concerns, and can even take advantage of a rather difficult situation. It is only a matter of time before you discover that a tricky problem is about to find an answer and you will be pleased to do some serious thinking for a friend.

Your lucky numbers this week: 3, 14, 26, 30.

12–18 FEBRUARY 2000

You are in a good mood and your energy level is high. If you want to achieve something special this is a good time to look for change. The weekend could be wonderful. If you are invited out by a member of the opposite sex, be sure to make a good impression and take advantage of it.

Your lucky numbers this week: 11, 22, 33, 34.

19–25 FEBRUARY 2000

Make a special effort to clear the dead wood out of your life this week. Unwanted friendships and acquaintances should be terminated in order to make way for new people to enter your life. You will benefit from advice of a stranger this weekend. Pay attention during casual conversations.

Your lucky numbers this week: 21, 23, 25, 36.

26 FEBRUARY–3 MARCH 2000

What happens at work this week will upset your expectations for months ahead. You may have to lower your sights temporarily. Do not let this disillusion you, however, for things will work out to your advantage. This weekend is a bad time for romance. Partners are likely to be difficult and argumentative.

Your lucky numbers this week: 1, 13, 17, 30.

4–10 MARCH 2000

With potentially exciting things going on in all areas of life this week, there is nothing to prevent you from being cheerful and positive in your approach to life. Not everyone is inclined to agree with you at present, but you can bring almost anyone round to your point of view this week.

Your lucky numbers this week: 11, 12, 23, 34.

11–17 MARCH 2000

You may have been having some trouble sorting out relationships. The balance can be restored now. This is an excellent period for getting on the right wavelength with your partner. You will find loved ones prepared to see your point of view.

Your lucky numbers this week: 5, 17, 19, 30.

18–24 MARCH 2000

Do not take anything or anyone for granted. You will find relatives rather unpredictable. Your partner may not wish to follow through with plans agreed for this week, even though you previously asked their opinion and made the arrangements.

Your lucky numbers this week: 1, 17, 20, 34.

25–31 MARCH 2000

Much care is needed when handling money. Do not allow your recent success to go to your head. Stick with your present lifestyle. You may wish to act like a big shot. Do not throw your money around, trying to make a good impression.

Your lucky numbers this week: 2, 5, 32, 33.

1 APRIL–7 APRIL 2000

As long as you have not set your sights too high, this can be a reasonably successful week. Set aside time to deal with financial affairs. Those of you who require co-operation from others to achieve satisfactory work should try to improve the atmosphere.

Your lucky numbers this week: 2, 3, 14, 26.

8–14 APRIL 2000

Travel will bring good results. You will probably feel like a change of environment this week, and be grateful for any opportunities to meet new people. Routine matters will have little appeal now. You will be keen to get on with exciting new plans this week.

Your lucky numbers this week: 13, 14, 29, 33.

15–21 APRIL 2000

Do not spend too much time on run-of-the-mill jobs. It is import-ant to allow the creative side of your nature more freedom. Be creative, and let your natural talents breathe. Long-distance matters continue to be lucrative.

Your lucky numbers this week: 12, 23, 26, 30.

22–28 APRIL 2000

This will be a fairly slow, uneventful week business-wise. It may be frustrating to have to complete a deal after the weekend, but it would be extremely unwise to be too pushy. You could lose a valuable contact if you try to force things now.

Your lucky numbers this week: 3, 17, 19, 34.

29 APRIL–5 MAY 2000

As far as business goes, you should be on the ball. You will start this week in fine form and have no problems when it comes to dealing with colleagues. Your power of intuition should be good. The week also bodes well for romantic affairs.

Your lucky numbers this week: 12, 23, 34, 36.

6–12 MAY 2000

Arguments over insignificant issues are likely at home. Married Pigs in particular will have to watch their tempers. Do not be overly critical of your partner and try not to interfere in the way family members are handling their work. Do not take a bossy or dictatorial attitude.

Your lucky numbers this week: 5, 17, 19, 30.

13–19 MAY 2000

This should be a happy and successful week for socializing. Pay more attention to pleasure than to regular work. It is likely that you have been ignoring the wishes of your family to some degree; do all that you can to remedy the situation now. There will be opportunities to work on valuable creative projects but they should not interfere with romantic moments with your chosen one.

Your lucky numbers this week: 1, 4, 20, 35.

20–26 MAY 2000

Nothing of any great significance is likely during this rather quiet week. This is not a good week for making a long journey and avoid activities with large groups of people. Do what you can to make this period a pleasant week for your immediate family.

Your lucky numbers this week: 1, 5, 17, 19, 33.

27 MAY–2 JUNE 2000

You need to tread warily, for there are a number of pitfalls to look out for. The cash situation requires careful handling. Numerous regular bills are now due, and you may find your reserves falling rather drastically. However a letter received this week should bring good news.

Your lucky numbers this week: 2, 4, 15, 26.

3–9 JUNE 2000

The domestic sphere continues to soak up much of your time. You may plan to spend more time with your closest ones this week. Meanwhile you need to deal with various practical matters in a way that allows you to continue with them next week in a more positive way.

Your lucky numbers this week: 13, 24, 26, 27.

10–16 JUNE 2000

Life this week seems a lot easier. Your mature outlook on life helps you to tackle practical matters and even turn difficult situations to your own advantage. You will discover that an especially tricky problem is about to be resolved and you will be happy to put your thinking cap on for the benefit of a friend.

Your lucky numbers this week: 15, 17, 19, 32.

17–23 JUNE 2000

A good week for reorganizing things within your working environment. Do not be deterred by the complaints of colleagues, as you are doing things the right way. Superiors will be easy to approach. Domestic affairs may not be running smoothly yet, so discussions with partners could help to remedy this state of affairs.

Your lucky numbers this week: 1, 5, 20, 33.

24–30 JUNE 2000

Start the week as you mean to carry on. This is not a good day for changes, so set your goals and keep your eyes on them. You may find that you are burdened with the problems of a colleague. Be strong enough to hand them back if they are too much for you. Romantic matters are improving.

Your lucky numbers this week: 5, 17, 19, 31.

1 JULY–7 JULY 2000

Caution is required when operating anything mechanical or electrical. There is a danger of accidents. Be careful about experimenting with any gadget you do not understand. Read instructions carefully before tampering with instruments totally unknown to you. The best part of the week comes from Wednesday onwards. You will not want to stray far from home.

Your lucky numbers this week: 8, 18, 20, 31.

8–14 JULY 2000

Do not allow colleagues to take advantage of your good nature, especially where cash loans are involved. Lending money now will lead to complications later when you try to retrieve it. A failed romance can be healed this weekend.

Your lucky numbers this week: 2, 17, 29, 30.

15–21 JULY 2000

This is not a good period for business. You are unlikely to communicate successfully with the right people. There may have been some recent celebrations involving your colleagues, who have unfortunately not yet got back into the habit of working. However, you can count on a breakthrough at the end of the week, when everything will turn out right for you. Your present relationship will receive a boost.

Your lucky numbers this week: 12, 23, 25, 34.

22–28 JULY 2000

You may be feeling uncertain about progress in your career. If you are at all unhappy with things as they are, consult superiors to ascertain your next move. Finances could have a small boost midweek. Romance develops along familiar lines this week, though not necessarily in a way to your liking.

Your lucky numbers this week: 1, 5, 17, 32.

29 JULY–4 AUGUST 2000

You have to be on your toes this week. Being quick-witted, you are not usually deceived by other people, but someone you thought you could trust may be out to make a fool of you in one way or another. A longstanding colleague may wish to borrow money, but do not lend cash without being sure of exactly how and when you are going to get it back. If you do not cover yourself where it counts, you could end up losing out. Devote time to creative work that gives you the opportunity to use your fertile imagination.

Your lucky numbers this week: 3, 14, 25, 35.

5–11 AUGUST 2000

Imagination and intuition can be turned to good use this week. Make notes about any creative ideas and keep them for future reference. Those involved in creative jobs should have an excellent week, packed full of originality. Hunches should be acted upon. Try out new ideas.

Your lucky numbers this week: 5, 17, 19, 31.

12–18 AUGUST 2000

This is a good week to complete outstanding business. Clear away routine work and deal with more important items as soon as possible. Do not let stick-in-the mud colleagues stand in your way. Your judgement is fairly good at present, so follow your instincts.

Your lucky numbers this week: 1, 17, 19, 34.

19–25 AUGUST 2000

Things at your place of work should be going in your favour and you may have the power to change things permanently. Financially, this is not a good week for taking gambles or getting involved in anything of a speculative nature. Keep your cash in your own pocket wherever possible.

Your lucky numbers this week: 2, 27, 29, 36.

26 AUGUST–1 SEPTEMBER 2000

Romance goes through a specially rocky time this week. Permanent partnerships will also encounter problems. If you find yourself attracted to a member of the opposite sex, make certain that your initial feelings are sound. This is not a time to put relationships in jeopardy.

Your lucky numbers this week: 5, 17, 19, 31.

2–8 SEPTEMBER 2000

A working week that drags by slowly. Routine matters seem to be unnecessarily difficult and you are thwarted by busybodies. Try not to lose your temper as you will come out the worse for wear if you become involved in arguments. Confrontations with spouses should also be avoided.

Your lucky numbers this week: 3, 18, 20, 30.

9–15 SEPTEMBER 2000

It is time to give your career plans a push. Set things in motion this week for best effect, and do not allow weaker colleagues to stand in your way. Romantic encounters in your work environment take on a note of seriousness. Make certain that your intended is not already spoken for.

Your lucky numbers this week: 1, 17, 19, 32.

16–22 SEPTEMBER 2000

Money matters require cautious handling. Pigs must be careful about whom they are dealing with. Speculation in any form would be most hazardous. You will have a tendency to be careless with money, so keep personal spending within reasonable limits and guard your wallet.

Your lucky numbers this week: 2, 5, 26, 27.

23–29 SEPTEMBER 2000

Home and property affairs are badly starred this week. You could find yourself making a big mistake where a new house or a move is concerned so avoid signing contracts and make no financial commitments. This weekend will find you in pensive mood. Do not make partners' lives a misery.

Your lucky numbers this week: 3, 5, 26, 27.

30 SEPTEMBER–6 OCTOBER 2000

Bury yourself in your work early this week, dealing with routine matters before midweek. There will be much to do later. Enlist the help of an older colleague should you find it necessary. Younger members of the staff may try to stop you getting what you want. Do nothing this weekend that could lead to gossip.

Your lucky numbers this week: 5, 17, 19, 30.

7–13 OCTOBER 2000

You may not be thinking straight about money. It would be extremely dangerous to make new investments now. Expert advice will cost little and could eliminate risks. New business propositions must be carefully investigated. Be wary about getting too deeply involved with people you meet for the first time, and try to avoid becoming too emotional.

Your lucky numbers this week: 6, 28, 29, 33.

14–20 OCTOBER 2000

Speculation could still be your downfall. The temptation to invest in the propositions of friends will be very strong. Keep your impulses in check. It is wise to look before you leap. At times of uncertainty, consult your partner if in need of advice. Single Pigs will experience a romantic period this week.

Your lucky numbers this week: 5, 17, 19, 34.

21–27 OCTOBER 2000

You might feel that you are short of cash at present. This could cause you to stop and think about the more significant expenses in your life. Perhaps you could do a little reorganizing and make cash go further than it does currently. New incentives probably arise at work.

Your lucky numbers this week: 1, 5, 17, 32.

28 OCTOBER–3 NOVEMBER 2000

You may have to change your plans for this week to avoid serious arguments. Although you might feel that people are behaving irrationally, they will be calling the tune. Co-operation will be difficult, though this is a good week for jobs that let you show your artistic prowess, especially if you can handle them alone.

Your lucky numbers this week: 6, 7, 19, 33.

4–10 NOVEMBER 2000

Travel plans for this week should be postponed. This is not a good time to make long journeys, whether for business or for pleasure. If you cannot avoid them, then be particularly cautious when driving. Be careful when driving and check your car before setting out.

Your lucky numbers this week: 1, 18, 19, 32.

11–17 NOVEMBER 2000

An extremely happy week for activities around the home. There will be good opportunities for building upon your relationship with your partner. Unacknowledged disagreements can now be discussed for everyone's benefit. An engagement this week is likely to lead to a happy marriage.

Your lucky numbers this week: 8, 17, 29, 35.

18–24 NOVEMBER 2000

You will have some difficulty understanding the impulsive actions of loved ones. Ideas you had about making changes in your home may not be acceptable to them. It is also possible that someone is trying to pull the wool over your eyes. Work will be relatively simple compared to your domestic situation. This is a good week for experimenting with the way you work.

Your lucky numbers this week: 5, 17, 19, 32.

25 NOVEMBER–1 DECEMBER 2000

It is quite likely that the problem of loves ones will interfere with your own plans. A member of your family may not be feeling too well so it might be necessary to cancel reservations. Do not be too disappointed if entertainment plans have to be postponed at the last minute.

Your lucky numbers this week: 2, 17, 32, 34.

2–8 DECEMBER 2000

Emotionally this could be one of the most upsetting weeks that Pigs have confronted for some time. Those of you who are single will be worrying about the progress of a relationship. Parents will be particularly concerned for their children's welfare.

Your lucky numbers this week: 15, 18, 19, 33.

9–15 DECEMBER 2000

You should be prepared to take chances this week. You will be in harmony with a work colleague and joint ventures will be fruitful. Domestic partnerships may suffer from a lack of attention on your part, and romance is also going through a sticky period.

Your lucky numbers this week: 5, 17, 19, 31.

16–22 DECEMBER 2000

Work will be fun this week. The atmosphere at your workplace will be conducive to producing results. Colleagues are willing to follow any lead that you give and new ideas you have been waiting to put into action can now be attempted successfully.

Your lucky numbers this week: 8, 17, 19, 32.

23–29 DECEMBER 2000

Look out for arguments, as combined influences in your chart create a more argumentative Pig than has been the case of late. In reality you have few of the answers and must allow differences of opinion. In many respects the week is quite happy; in the end it really depends on you.

Your lucky numbers this week: 15, 17, 19, 32.

30 DECEMBER–5 JANUARY 2001

Disagreements with your partner will easily develop. These may arise because of what occurred last week. Plans suggested to you are unlikely to be acceptable, and you will be quite pleased to get away from the domestic environment this week.

Your lucky numbers this week: 12, 17, 20, 33.

6–12 JANUARY 2001

Freedom from pressures lets you do as you please. Personal relationships will be much on your mind. You will be keen to iron out differences with loved ones. This can be done with frank, calm discussions where nobody loses their temper. You will probably be in the mood for mixed company.

Your lucky numbers this week: 1, 19, 32, 35.

13–19 JANUARY 2001

This week you have a feeling of inadequacy, as well as vague doubts and fears that have no secure foundation – these are handicaps from which you may suffer this week. Influential people may be difficult to please, though this is no reason to worry about your own performance.

Your lucky numbers this week: 17, 19, 22, 33.

20–26 JANUARY 2001 (24 JANUARY: CHINESE NEW YEAR – YEAR OF THE SNAKE)

Face up boldly to what has to be done. Do not try to wriggle out of your responsibilities and throw yourself into your job. There is no way to solve your financial problems through gambling. Once you understand what is bothering you, coping with it will not be that difficult.

Your lucky numbers this week: 1, 17, 19, 32.

AUTHOR'S NOTE

I have held many courses and seminars about Chinese fortune-telling, and I have also written about this subject in newspapers and magazines. This is my first book about Chinese
astrology in English and I hope you will have great pleasure
sharing my knowledge as you read this book. I thank Element
Books for being so good as to publish this book.

HENNING HAI LEE YANG

FOR FURTHER INFORMATION

if you would like to have your Chinese horoscope compiled or
have a face- or palm-reading by one of the world's most com-
petent fortune-tellers, please do not hesitate to contact Henning Hai Lee Yang for further information. He can give you
information in five different languages and can be contacted
at the following address:

Henning Hai Lee Yang
Brugaten 1
0186 Oslo
Norway
Tel: (47) 221 77250
Fax: (47) 221 50542
E-mail: yang@yangz.com
Http: //www.yangz.com

Henning Hai Lee Yang has also devised the Hai Lee *I Ching*
oracle-system which is based on the *I Ching*, the 'Book of
Changes'. The *I Ching* is an ancient source of wisdom which

the Chinese have consulted for over 5000 years. The *I Ching* system is based on trigrams that create a total of 64 different combinations. Each combination has its own meaning and offers an amazing answer to whatever question is put to it. It can be consulted about virtually anything – from questions on love, health and wealth to information about lucky numbers and lost objects.

To consult the Hai Lee *I Ching* oracle-system:

- Think of a question
- Call 0906 6409190 (calls charged at standard rate of £1 per minute)
- Dial a number randomly between 01 and 64
- The *I Ching* will give you the answer